Me and Jamie

By

Raymond F. Rogers

ISBN: 1-40331-387-3

This book is printed on acid free paper.

1st Books - rev. 05/02/02

Table of Contents

FORWARD

I have enjoyed writing "Me and Jamie". I have written at a rapid pace, unshackled by the usual rules of grammar, and it has been fun. I suspect that a great part of the fun has come from this freedom, because I usually must labor very hard to express ideas. Even at my age, I remain very doubtful concerning the rules of punctuation, I am not a great speller, and I make mistakes. To assume, ahead of time, forgiveness for my errors is a pleasure. If this should fall into the hands of someone who finds this presumption unacceptable, that person has my apology; but I will not prostrate myself before his disapproval. I am not so cavalier, however, about another device that I have used rather freely: that of sexual humor. It seemed to come very naturally to me, in speaking through an adolescent, to feel released from the usual moral constraints that should attend the efforts of a sixty-two year old grandfather.

If some find that these pages contain nothing more than the feeble attempts of a bluenose to provide sexual humor, I accept the charge. If some, on the other hand, find parts of these pages offensive, I sincerely apologize for the offence and hope that the person offended will read the remainder of this introduction.

I plead guilty with an explanation. Human sexuality produces a dilemma for the morally circumspect person in today's society. I cannot, nor do I attempt in this little book, to solve this dilemma. I refuse, however, to perpetuate a long held custom of ignoring the fact that growing boys and girls are faced with difficult choices in their adolescence. Our progeny bear ample evidence that we are sexual creatures. We love our children. It is my belief that it is never healthy for them to feel that we deplore the act that brought them into existence. I believe also that, in the context of marriage, sexual pleasure should be as accessible to the saint as to the sinner.

Since some who may see this have children for whom they are responsible, I commend them should they question whether what is read or seen might make chastity more difficult for children. If God has put the welfare of youngsters into your hands, I wish you Godspeed.

Should you elect to read this little book before placing it into the hands of your charges, please do not complain that the contents are no more stimulating than this introduction. Children who watch television, as well as adults, may have become too sophisticated to find any humor in my naïve attempts. If, however, your mind can be transported to a more innocent era, you may reward my efforts with a smile.

I wish you to laugh with me some, smile with me some, and, since I'm wishing, think a bit.

Most of the characters you will meet here exist only in the mind. I have endeavored to make them believable. I believe the fictional characters could have existed along with the real ones I have included.

The episode of the lost apple was very real. I used the real names of my mother and her siblings. I cannot know what happened beyond what Mother told me. I think what I wrote could have been the way it was.

More than one reader has found Frankie's vocabulary to be too extensive for his years. I have chosen to leave the precocious boy as I found him, simply to make him more interesting. If I took away either the bad grammar or the uses to which Frankie put new words, I am afraid I might lose your attention. Please indulge me.

I hope you will enjoy my little book.

Raymond F. Rogers

Greensboro, N.C.

January, 1987 Revised, 2002

CASUAL IN CASWELL

This book is about a boy's growing up in a farming community in North Carolina. I am the one who wrote the narratives and various essays in the book, but I am no longer a boy.

Most of the contents of this book conform very closely to the frequent entries I made in my writing tablets, before I became convinced that to use correct grammar is a desirable goal for one who seeks to express ideas.

As some of the entries in the book make clear, Jamie and I deliberately used poor grammar, believing it to be a mark of our maleness. It is rather curious that we were so defiant on that point and so careful to obey other rules.

This book would most certainly not have been written without the encouragement of my wife. If I could somehow reveal to you the commitment that Gladys has to the proper uses of the English language, you would better understand the depth of her love for me. She insists that the entries in my old writing tablets be copied very much as written. She says that the "flavor" of them is better preserved this way. Gladys has assisted in getting the papers in order. Even she did not insist that my spelling needed no improvement. She helped me with the spelling to make the book easier to read. She thought we should leave some of the words as written. You will note that many words are wrong, but fairly consistent.

As a boy, I spelled words more like they are spoken. Here in our county we rarely sound the "g" at the end of words. The book will usually show these words correctly spelled. We retained my old spellings for library, widow, fellow, and such.

The poor grammar remains in the book at Gladys' insistence. The grammar is less consistent than the spelling. I made a few gradual adjustments in my grammar as I was growing up. I made dramatic changes when my teacher convinced my mother that I should. I believe the contents will explain about this.

I have sufficient respect for my wife's judgment not to make more corrections. She says that, as written, the feelings of a growing boy are revealed with greater clarity with the words of the boy retained.

Please do not conclude that all natives of Caswell County speak like Jamie and I did. We were notoriously bad and enjoyed the notoriety.

Benjamin Franklin Friddle
Caswell Country 2002

ESSAY

Franklin Benjamin Friddle English Period Grade 5

This is a SA. A SA is more fun than to write on a subject where you have to go to the liberry and look up things. I look up things here at my desk. This is a lot more fun than to go to the liberry, where the teacher goes, "Shush," and takes your name down, just because you go, "Ouch!" when Jamie Klinghopper jabs you in the behind with a pencil. The teachers in the liberry expect us lively boys to act as quiet as the girls and the sissy boys.

Two boys in our room is so sissy they get a "A" in deportment, just like the girls. I don't call the names of no sissies, out of respect for their folks. There ain't no use shaming whole families, just because one boy in that bunch ain't got enough spunk to rattle a teacher's decorum often enough to avoid getting a "A" in deportment. Me and Jamie ain't no sissies.

If me and Jamie was to go back to Old Lady Showalter's room without our names being took down by the teacher whose turn it is to grade papers in the liberry, Miss Showalter would surmise we had skipped liberry period. Every one of them teachers is real anxious to have it quiet in the liberry. Once even Rosemary Raincamp had to leave the liberry, when she had the hiccups.

This is not a SA on the liberry. This is a SA on how to write a SA. Teacher says that when you write a SA, you write about what you know. This is going to be easy, and I know it is going to be fun; because what I

3

know would fill a brook (like, what I know will flow out of my head and onto my paper – like a brook).

Still, it is a lot more fun to just think about things than to write them down on a silly old piece of gray paper, with blue lines to keep you from running everything together, with this old pencil that just about got chewed in two by the dog.

It is especially fun to look up things here at my school desk.

When you write a SA, you are supposed to use some "similes". I know how to spell "simile", because the teacher has got it wrote on the blackboard, where all of us can see it, so we will remember to say that something is like something, and the something it is like is not exactly like what you say it is like. The more unlike it is, to the something that you say it is like, the better the simile.

Boy, have I got a good way to remember that! "Simile" sounds like, "see Nellie's". But it is not the same as to see Nellie's at all!

Sometimes, if I scrunch down just right, I can see Gladys'. This is a lot more fun than "see Nellie's". And, even if they were Nellie's, it would be more fun to see them on Gladys. So I can remember what "simile" means, even if Old Lady Showalter didn't have it wrote on the blackboard. (Sometimes I might tell you how I remember "Showalter".)

When you write a SA, you are supposed to write "off the top of your head". Like, when dandruff falls off the top of your head. When I say that my ideas fall from my head like dandruff, I don't mean that my ideas are flaky, I mean my ideas are like dandruff only become they come from my head. My thoughts sometimes scatter like dandruff, but they are usually worth a lot more than dandruff – so this must be a good simile. (My ideas are sure a whole lot better than Jamie Klinghopper's was when he got a bunch of us in a whole lot of trouble last Halloween.)

This is not a SA on "simile" either, but I will tell you one more thing about it. You can sometimes use a simile, if you say something is as something as something else, even when it is not as pretty as, or as big as, or as small as something: just so you can kind of draw a picture of the something it is as something as (but not really). Like, I could say, "Mary's is as pretty as Gladys', but that would not be a simile; that would be comparison. (And, it would not be true, because nobody's is as pretty as Gladys'.) If I say that Mary's is as white as snow; that might be a simile, but it would not be true. I could say that Mary's is as white as Jamie Klinghopper's handkerchief, which he has been carrying around, like a security blanket for his nose, since he was six years old. That might be a simile, and it would be true; but Teacher says that similes should sound nice.

Old Lady Showalter says that a SA should have a "kick" on the end, so it will be remembered by anybody that might read it. She said, too, that we should "rewrite". She has got "kick" and "rewrite", wrote on the blackboard, too. (She has got a list of words to help us as we write our SA. Right at the top, she has got "essay", whatever that means. Nobody has asked her about it, and I sure ain't!)

I'll write this over, when I look up how to spell some words; and I'll change some other things, so she won't know what I've been doing sometimes when it looked like I was concentrating real hard.

Writing a SA is a lot like writing on "assigned topics", except you get to look up what you want to.

I'm about ready to finish my SA, if I can find the "kick" for it. I think I'll just scrunch down here – and think about it. Oh boy! Gladys has nothing on her mind but her SA. What a kick!

McELWAINE'S GOAT

One day when me and Jamie Klinghopper was playing mumblety-peg at recess, while most of the girls and some sissy boys was playing dodge ball, we saw Old Man McElwaine's billy goat climb up the wooden steps and go into the school hall. Jamie said, if Old Lady Showalter sees that goat in the school house, she'll wet her pants."

Now, I ain't one to worry none about the sogginess of the teacher's drawers, but I was concerned about how crotchety she'd be if she had a accident all because of Old Man McElwaine's billy goat. Besides, I usually went along with anything Jamie wanted to do as long as it increased the action. And there just ain't that much action in mumblety-peg.

We both got up right away from where we were squatting in the shade of some big oaks. Jamie pocketed his Barlow knife and I folded my Blue Steel Wonder and put it in the pocket that didn't have a hole in it and started after Jamie who was already headed at a slow trot toward the wooden steps of the school.

We both wanted to catch that goat before a puddle formed under the teacher's chair. Now if you ain't never heard a goat walk across a wooden floor, you don't have no idea what we was up against trying to keep Old Lady Showalter from finding out about that billy goat.

Where we had been playing mumblety-peg was about as far from the school house steps as Luther Murray can throw a baseball. Luther can chunk a rock harder and throw a baseball farther than anybody you ever saw.

We was far enough that by the time we went into the hall we couldn't see that billy goat nowheres – and you could see all the way through the hall to the other end.

Me and Jamie looked at each other to see if either him or me had any idea of what to do next. We both knowed that most of the teachers would be outside on a day like today. The teachers took turns being playground monitor. Which just means that they knowed on each day who would stop fights and who would stop Earl Junior's nose from bleeding. All the other teachers would sit around the picnic table and grade papers, talk teacher's talk, or gossip about the young preacher over to the Methodist Church and how the organist had taken a new interest in her dress and manners.

But we knowed for sure that Old Lady Showalter had stayed inside to read and grade the SA's that we had wrote the day before. It was a hot day, so all the classroom doors was open. That billy goat could be anywheres – in any classroom or cloakroom or, for all we knowed, clean out the other end of the hall.

But we really didn't think the goat had run that far because if it had Old Lady Showalter would have been out in the hall to take down the name of whoever was running in the schoolhouse.

We didn't say all this to each other. We both just knowed that the other knowed enough about billy goats and teachers that that was the way it was. Some things boys like me and Jamie don't have to learn in no classroom.

Jamie took one side of the hall while I took the other. I went into Old Lady Crookshank's room and he went into Old Lady Cunningham's. Both of us made quick runs around the empty classrooms and cloakrooms, imagining what Old Man McElwaine's goat would do to the lunches if he found a way to get to any. We'd worked our way about half way through the school when we both saw the billy goat come out of our classroom. He still had something in his mouth he had been chewing on, and the teacher tried to catch him by the tail just as he got out of the doorway. When she saw us, Old Lady Showalter let go of the goat's tail and ducked back into the classroom.

The billy goat ran on through the hall and out the back door, sounding like when you run a stick against the Pickering's Picket fence on the way home from the barbershop. We walked after the goat. We didn't want to be accused of running in the hall. That old goat just ambled into the pen at Old Man McElwaine's just as we reached the door and Luther rang the big bell for the end of morning recess.

When we got back to the classroom, our teacher was sitting at her desk with our papers scattered about on the floor. The teacher's face was red, trying to turn purple, (or maybe it was turning from purple back to red.) She tried a few times to say something, but she didn't make a sound except kind of choking like, and she motioned that me and Jamie and the others should gather up the papers.

It didn't take long to get the papers together because we knowed that we were not supposed to see the marks on each other's papers. We just made a pile of them on her desk.

We couldn't see enough to make sure about Jamie's forecast concerning the teacher's lack of control. We started believing he had been right though when the teacher backed up to the blackboard and wrote, kind of over her shoulder with a new piece of chalk. What she wrote was

"E-S-S-A-Y." She just stood there for a long time as the color of her face came back to its usual plainness.

When she was able finally to speak, she said, "Although the word 'essay, E-S-S-A-Y' is pronounced the same as 'S A, capital S, capital A', it should not be written that way."

She said that the only way she wanted to see SA on any essay was a essay on South America. When she said something like that she usually said, "Ha, ha!"

I guess the reason she didn't say, "Ha, ha", this time was that she didn't want the wet spot on the back of her dress to get any bigger.

Old Lady Showalter sat back down and we didn't do much more in class that the teacher would need to stand up to do. So far as I know, she stayed right at her desk through lunch time and afternoon recess.

I got a C+ on my essay. I was lucky to get that considering all the red marks for spelling mistakes and all the time I got essay wrong. I found out later that she only counted a mistake once, no matter how many times it was wrote.

Jamie got a "C-". This was the best grade Jamie ever got on a English paper. Jamie don't know how to use proper grammar like me and Rosemary Raincamp. But Jamie's real smart in most ways that count.

That afternoon Jamie and me hightailed it over to Old Man McElwaine's goat pen as soon as school was out. Considering what we found in the pen, it don't take no Sherlock Holmes to figure out what happened that day, when me and Jamie was trying so hard to head off that billy goat.

There, all trampled down into the muck of that goat pen, was a pair of chewed-up bloomers. They was in too bad a shape to tell anything about the size, but you could still make out some blue color under all of that goat manure.

You might not be able to prove it over to the Yanceyville Courthouse, but me and Jamie knowed who it was that spent the biggest part of the day on a wet chair without no bloomers.

One thing I knowed for sure was that them blue bloomers wasn't wore by Nellie and they sure wasn't Gladys'.

We laughed about that billy goat's trip through school. So far as we knowed, he was the only one that ever got all the way through school in one day. Me and Jamie also think he was the only one to go through school that got into Old Lady Showalter's drawers.

REBECCA FARTHINGTON

There was a real pretty woman that stayed at Thacker's Boarding House. She was about the most exciting woman in the whole town. I still don't know why, but me and Jamie would both watch her as long as we could when she walked down Maple Street. I never had it put to the test, as grown-ups say, but I suspicion that if this lady and Gladys should walk by the barber shop going in opposite directions on Maple Street I would let Gladys walk away unwatched for once. That woman was sure pretty and swelled out in the nicest places.

She had a fancy name, Rebecca Farthington. The men in town would refer to her as "Becky", but a whole lot of the women got to calling her "that hussy". I don't know what that means, but it must not be nice. They say it in the same tone of voice that Ma used that time when Tom, the cat, had been accidentally locked in the house while we was all away at the Grange picnic. Ma don't cuss, but the way she talked about what that cat had done on her best shawl would have put a cusser to shame.

I heard a part of the conversation some of the ladies had when they met at our house for Ma's circle. I perked up and got as close as I could without nobody paying no attention to me when I heard somebody say the name, "Miss Farthington", in a voice that was too nice to mean nice. They said that she was a woman of "easy virtue".

Now, there ain't nobody that knows everything about everything, but between me and Jamie, we know enough about most things that we can kind of get a handle on what's happening. We were both puzzled about the "easy virtue" business. Up to now I had understood that virtue was something that everybody wanted for themselves. If not for themselves, they surely wanted it for their children. I knowed it because I was going with Ma to prayer meeting on Wednesday night since I was knee high to a bench legged beagle, and I don't know how many times I heard Ma and them other women praying earnestly for the virtue of their children. If virtue is so hard to come by for most of us, why were the women of Ma's circle upset that pretty Miss Rebecca Farthington found virtue so easy?

Part of the puzzlement that me and Jamie felt was because we knowed that our Ma's didn't care a hill of beans for that "floozy", but we also knowed that Becky had a special attraction for us – and it turned out, for about every other male in the county.

I figured that why it was, was that the women didn't trust no good looking woman that was prettier than any of them or their daughters, especially if that "fine figure of a woman" came from as far away as Norfolk.

One time I was in the barber shop and all of the men was talking about things like the cost of seed and fertilizer, or the farm agent over to Yanceyville, when Miss Rebecca Farthington walked by. Boy, you would have thought that Sally Rand had just dropped her fan on the sidewalk outside the shop. Every eye in the place was turned toward the window. And three of the men went to the door to get a better view, as Becky walked along Maple Street. I would have gone to the door myself, but I was in the barber chair with that sheet tied over me so that I wouldn't get hairs down my neck that would cause me to itch until I had a bath the next Saturday.

Becky was sure a fine looking lady. Life in our part of the country was a lot more fun with her living over to Thacker's Boarding House.

One place that I never saw Miss Farthington was over to the church. Some of the boys in school went to the Methodist Church and they said that she didn't go there either. I figured that if she wasn't a Baptist or a Methodist, she might go into Yanceyville for Sunday services – but maybe all Rebecca Farthington did on Sunday mornings was to sleep late in her room at Thacker's Boarding House.

I think I found out why it was that Miss Farthington didn't go to church. She knowed that she would not be welcomed. This is another puzzle that me and Jamie worked on along with some of the other boys at school. All of us boys enjoyed talking about Miss Becky.

It was at another of Ma's circle meetings that I found out about the overhaul of the welcome mats down to the Baptist and Methodist Churches. I heard things like, "I wouldn't want that woman under the same roof with my husband." And then, "or any of my boys." Female voices carry very good at our house, especially if a feller keeps his ears tuned to the right station.

I found out that what sparked this discussion about the pretty Miss Becky was that old lady Crump had a sister in Danville that asked about a place for her husband to stay while he worked for a few weeks in our town. He was a sawmill operator and was going to be in town while old man Turner's timber was being harvested. Old lady Crump didn't have room for him at her house and had asked the other ladies what they thought about her brother-in-law staying at Mrs. Thacker's Boarding House.

What me and Jamie was so mixed up about was the two directions that them ladies was going at the same time. We had visitation nights down at the Baptist Church. And what we would do would be to go around and invite anybody new or anybody who had backslid to come to church on Sunday – because God loves everybody, including the Methodist and even the Presbyterians over to Yanceyville.

Why, them women even got old Zeb Tuttle sobered up for preaching service one Sunday last summer. If the town drunk was worth all that trouble, why did the women refuse to invite Miss Rebecca Farthington to Sunday services and to circle meetings?

Just because somebody has got "round heels" don't seem no reason to walk right by Mrs. Thacker's Boarding House on visitation nights. Me and Jamie has both looked at Becky's heels and we don't see nothing bad about them at all. In fact, if "round heels" is what Miss Rebecca Farthington had, all the women in the county ought to take up round-heel exercises, because Miss Becky had the prettiest heels you ever saw.

Anyway, going to preaching services would have been a lot more fun if you knowed you could look at Miss Becky between prayers. Shucks, I might have been lucky enough to have shared a song book with her, if that circle of old biddies didn't have this prejudice against pretty females that ain't no kin.

As for me, if I could have been sure of sharing a song book with Miss Rebecca Farthington, I would have even been willing to visit the Methodist Church. I think the Lord would have understood me forgetting about some fine points of doctrine when He saw how much I appreciated the fine job He did when He made Miss Farthington.

TELEGRAM

In his senior year Luther Murray got a job over to the Western Union. He didn't have to read Morse Code or nothing like that. He probably couldn't have done it. What Luther did was to take them telegrams to people who had just lost a grandma or grandpa or somebody and didn't even know it yet until Luther took them the little yellow envelopes.

Luther could ride a bicycle faster and farther without getting tuckered than anybody else in the county. Most everybody had to get off and push up Lineberry Hill, but not Luther. He rode that bicycle right up any hill like it was no problem at all.

The people at Western Union must have been mighty pleased to have Luther Murray to deliver their telegrams for there was nobody that ever finished deliveries as quick as Luther could on his Western Flyer.

With Luther delivering telegrams, shucks, folks could start grieving a whole lot sooner than they could have if Jeff Peabody was still the delivery man.

I heard that sometimes in a big city a telegram might bring good news. If it ever happened in our town, I never did hear about it. There was one though that wasn't bad news.

Some of the men over to the barber shop made it up that they would get Luther to deliver a telegram to Miss Becky Farthington at Mrs. Thacker's Boarding House. Well, they must have figured that was a pretty good joke because those telegrams cost money. But they made it up between enough men that it didn't cost nobody much.

Grown-ups don't share much with small boys, but "little pitchers have big ears", so I was able to pick up a little of what the telegram had to say: "YOU EXCITE ME STOP YOU MAKE ME WANT TO MARRY YOU DON'T STOP - LUTHER MURRAY."

On the day that old man Farham sent the telegram, there was always some of the men that was in on the joke somewheres close to Mrs. Thacker's. Charlie Applewhite had some vegetables still left on his pickup after he sold all he could at Pickard's Grocery Store and at the Ivory Store. He parked near Thacker's Boarding House so he could see what was about to happen and no one would suspicion but what he was trying to sell his corn and tomatoes.

Charlie Applewhite went back to the barber shop about supper time that evening and reported that Luther was not at Thacker's Boarding House five minutes. Charlie said that when Luther rode up and went inside the boarding house, he didn't hardly have that bicycle fixed on its kick stand until he was already inside the house. Charlie was still debating with himself whether to follow Luther to Miss Becky's room when Luther came back out and was off again on his bicycle.

Naturally, I was curious as anybody about what would happen between Luther and Miss Becky. What I did was to go to the barber shop to sell my *Liberty* magazines. Besides getting to share in the excitement of the big joke, I got to make a few sales. Some of the fellows who couldn't spare a dime for a movie could raise a nickel for *Liberty*.

When Charlie made his report, such a pall fell over that shop, you would have thought that somebody's prize hound has just died. Nobody had ever thought that Luther wouldn't even be there when Miss Becky read the telegram about Luther wanting to marry her.

The way that joke flopped, the fellows in the barbershop must have felt the way some of those cocky batters feel when they've just been struck out again by Luther Murray's fast ball.

It wasn't long after the telegram joke that the school year ended and Luther graduated, without no special honors. I suspicion that Luther didn't hardly hear them fine graduation speeches about "broad vistas" and "new horizons". He probably had more important things on his mind because, within a week, we heard that Luther Murray and Rebecca Farthington had got married to each other over to the Presbyterian Church in Yanceyville.

Luther gave up his job with Western Union. He and his new bride set up housekeeping in Danville where Luther has got a new job making "Fruit of the Loom".

So the big joke had backfired and took a lot of the fun out of going to the barbershop, selling *Liberty* Magazines, or anything I used to do so I could watch Miss Becky Farthington walk that pretty way down Maple Street. A lot of life seems to have gone out of the barbershop crowd; but the women in the Circle are happy again, and back in love with everybody.

I guess it had to happen some time that some lucky bloke would marry Miss Becky. It couldn't have happened to a better fellow than Luther Murray. Luther ain't never fought nobody smaller than himself, which is everybody; he always kept the fire going in the potbellied stove in the school rooms where he was at in winter; he never made Earl Junior's nose bleed; and he rung the bell; and he lifted the log off of Freddie Blue's leg, where it fell when he went into the woods chasing the soccer ball that Jamie Klinghopper had just kicked a county mile. Shucks, I'm going to miss old Luther about as much as I will miss Miss Becky. Besides, Gladys Riddle is getting to be a lot like Miss Rebecca Farthington was. There ain't nobody getting to be nowhere near like Luther Murray was in keeping things going smooth over to the schoolhouse.

Fellers whose ma's don't belong to no circle don't have no idea how much a feller can learn while he is studying plane geometry in his room; if he'll just leave the door open while his ma's having circle meeting.

About half the boarders left Mrs. Thacker's when Miss Becky married and moved away to Danville. We found out that the reason Miss Becky had come from Norfolk in the first place, was to be the cook over at the boarding house. You would have thought that, with all the missionary work they did to find out that Luther and Becky's baby was born exactly ten months after their wedding day, somebody would have found out sooner what kind of work the pretty young woman from Norfolk was doing to support herself.

The Murrays named their new baby Charlie Farham Murray, after two of the fellers that worked out the joke with the telegram.

Me and Jamie liked Luther a lot. We still laugh a lot together at them smart dudes that shell out a quarter every Saturday afternoon so they can take a shower at the barbershop; put on the bay rum so they will smell good, and get a new shine on their fancy shoes for high stepping it out on Saturday nights. We laughed that all of them fellers missed out on courting Miss Becky.

19

It's as though old Luther Murray had rode off on his Western Flyer with the biggest prize in the county.

HARVESTERS

Saturday was a busy day at the barbershop. Mr. Crump would probably have had to hire somebody to cut hair in another chair if every other day was like Saturday. What he did was to hire Goofy Grogan to shine shoes and get the towels and soap to the dandies what came in to spruce up for their Saturday night shindigs.

If there was a little chill in the air, you could tell what day of the week it was by the sweat running down the storefront windows of Mr. Crump's shop. The trouble with the sweaty windows was that nobody could see the pretty girls walking down Maple Street to the Five and Ten or to the drug store. Another trouble with the sweaty windows was that mamas didn't find out as easy when to get supper ready, because you had to get all the way into the shop before you could tell how long it would be before Mr. Crump was going to get through cutting the hair of the one she was fixing supper for.

When the windows was clear, a lady could walk down the street opposite the shop and tell, as clear as you please, if it was about time to put the cornbread in the range. With the windows sweaty, you just couldn't see nothing in that shop from across the street. It would seem unladylike to step into the shop and just ask about the men. Besides, men folk don't want it known that their women keep such close tabs on them either.

There just ain't no telling how much topsoil went down the drain at Mr. Crump's barbershop. Some of the fellers worked at sawmills and would be dirty enough, with the pine rosin and all, but the really dirty ones would be the harvesters. You ain't seen dirty, until you've seen how much dirt will stick to the sweaty body of someone who is working with a combine at wheat harvest. Anyway, Old Man Crump got a lot of quarters from the men on the harvest crews.

After them men got a shave and haircut, a shower, some bay rum on their hair, a suit and tie, and fancy shoes, they was raring to go. With all the vinegar them bucks was feeling, you would never have guessed that they had just put in a fifty-six hour workweek in the wheat fields.

Me and Jamie has talked about it some, but we can't figger out how come them dandies was such a hot topic for the preachers on Sunday mornings. The way me and Jamie feels is that if these fellers has been working ten hours every day in the hot fields, they should be entitled to kick up their heels a little on a Saturday night.

Every year, just about the first or second Sunday after the wheat harvest begins, you can count on them dandies being raked over the coals by the preacher, because they have the gall to sleep late on Sunday mornings. We always sing, "Bringing In The Sheaves", and by the time the preacher is through talking about the danger them fellers is in, you just about feel like maybe you should rush right over to Thacker's Boarding House and roust them fellers out of bed and pull them into church, where the preacher could talk to the ones he was talking about.

I guess nobody ever thought to remind the preacher that for six of the seven days in the week them fellers had been in the field an hour before the preachers *Little Ben* alarm went off. I don't reckon any of them fellers ever said anything to the preacher about him sleeping late on six days to their one. Besides, I'm sure they know that the Lord rested on the seventh day.

Me and Jamie ain't sure, but we suspicion that what really riled the preacher was the good times them fellers had on Saturday nights.

Me and Jamie got to talking about this the other day, when we was down at Mabrey's mill pond fishing. There ain't enough fish in that pond to keep you busy all the time, so me and Jamie get to chew over a lot of things when we fish at Mabrey's Mill. Me and Jamie go to the same school and to the same church, and do a lot of things together, so we are more likely to come up on some pretty big things to be thought out at the same time.

Anyways, we was talking about how riled the preacher got over the harvest crew's Saturday night rambunctiousness, and we ain't got it all thought out yet, but what we did get worked out goes: if all of them fellers is "going to hell in a hand basket", ain't they in for a whole lot of suffering, so they shouldn't be begrudged a little bit of good-timing on a few Saturday nights?

All of us Baptists know that heaven lasts forever, and if the preacher and all of other Baptists, (and maybe a few Methodists and Presbyterians who mean well but just don't understand like us) if we are going to have eternal bliss, how come we are jealous of them dandies because they seem to have a good time when they get through working them long, hard days in the dusty fields. Maybe me and Jamie could be wrong about the preacher being jealous of them fellers for their "free and easy moral standards", but the way he keeps talking about it sure makes you think of the way Ma's circle carried on about that pretty Miss Rebecca Farthington.

Now it ain't that me and Jamie thinks it's alright to let those fellers go ahead and have a good time, if that means that they are "going to hell in a hand basket". That would be cruel, and we might have laughed when Alice Plunket slapped Earl Junior, and got his nose to bleeding, because of what he said about her "knockers", but me and Jamie ain't cruel. The way we figger is that it would be crueler to deprive them fellers of the only good times they will ever know. Why should we try to get them to sleep enough on Saturday nights so they can be rousted early enough on Sunday mornings, so's they can fill their bellies with hot biscuits, country ham, eggs, strawberry jam, and hot coffee, and still get down to the Baptist church in time to get yelled at with the rest of us, if this ain't going to keep them from going to hell. We figger it don't make no difference that they don't go in no hand basket – hell is hell.

Well this is about all the chewing we got done about the preacher and the harvesters. The fish finally started biting and we had enough pretty soon of sun perch and crappies for supper. But I ain't done thinking on it yet, and I believe I know Jamie Klinghopper well enough to figger that he'll think of something that'll put him over on the side of the fellers having a good time — if only because me and Jamie like to have a good time too.

Ma sure knows how to make a feller feel good about catching a mess of fish for supper. I won't repeat exactly what she said, it might sound like I was bragging, but what she said made me proud to take my Jim Bowie hunting knife and clean and dress the sun perch and crappies.

24

While I was out on the back porch cleaning the fish, Ma shredded some cabbage for slaw and made some hushpuppies. This way the big iron skillet was hot and ready when I brought the fish in ready for frying.

There just ain't many things as satisfying as feeling that your ma is really proud of you, especially if that satisfaction comes with a bellyful of fried fresh fish, slaw and hushpuppies that my ma has just cooked. Boy! I sure do love that woman.

After supper, when I had finished listening to Amos and Andy on my crystal radio set, I got to thinking again about the harvester men and the preacher. Maybe me and Jamie had come down too hard on the preacher. Maybe me and Jamie was just looking for a good excuse to maybe miss church some Sunday mornings, if we ever got big enough that we wouldn't get our hides tanned if we didn't go. I know that sometimes, because we want something to be so, it's easier to think it is so (like, the time I was so sure I had slid into home plate safe, because Cliff Turkle had plumb missed tagging me. I thought the umpire was as blind as a bat, until I found out that he was Gladys' brother).

I got out my Big Red writing tablet and made a list of things I thought might help me understand so's I wouldn't waste a good hate on the preacher. (A feller gets a lot more tolerant when he's about to say his prayers. Maybe the preacher thinks that he knows something that would keep them fellers from going to hell in a hand basket. The Christian thing to do is to tell them. How can he tell them if they are fast asleep on them soft pillows at Thacker's Boarding House every time he preaches?

HORNET

We kept fresh milk and butter in the springhouse. It was a nice little house, with a good tin roof and lattice work on the sides, so that air could get in, but not the foxes and coons, or Mr. McElwaine's goats that got out of the pen from time to time. It was fixed so the spring was right in the middle of the house, and the water ran from it out under the lattice work and on down a little branch. I don't remember that spring ever going completely dry, but it did slow to a trickle a few times. Folks in our county fancied our spring water as the sweetest around anywhere.

Pa had put a screen door spring on the door of the springhouse so the door wouldn't be left open. The spring was kind of in the midst of four tall tulip poplar trees, so the sun didn't hit the springhouse in the summertime, except in the very early mornings or in the late afternoons.

As the sun moved across the summer sky, the shadows of the big poplars would shorten and then lengthen again. I guess a lot of folks don't pay much attention to things like that, but maybe that's because they don't have a friend like Jamie Klinghopper for company, whilst they watch the bees, yellow jackets, and dirt daubers working the banks of the branch, right at the shadow line of the poplar trees.

Me and Jamie would watch as the construction workers of the insect world gather up building material from the clay which had been softened by the cool spring water. Of course I made a lot of trips down to the springhouse, to fetch water mostly, but sometimes, it would be to get butter for Ma's pound cakes or to bring back sweet milk to go with our cornbread for supper. I was at that springhouse a lot, and my eyes would naturally pick up where the dirt daubers was working — always at the shadow line of them poplars, except in the early mornings they would be working a little farther down the branch where the shade of the big oaks fell.

Me and Jamie would watch them insects for hours, and talk about things at the same time. Once in awhile, one of us would call attention to what a big load of mud a dirt dauber was about to take off with; then we'd go right back to whatever subject it was that was turning cartwheels in our minds.

One Saturday in late spring, when me and Jamie had been playing catch in the shade of the poplars, we laid down on our bellies, down below the springhouse, to rest our tired arms. We was both interested to see that some robins had also started to work in the softened clay.

It's funny how your thoughts can run on more than one track at the same time. What's even stranger is that me and Jamie would find out that we would think about the same things before either one of us had brought up those things to be chewed over. Anyways, while our eyes followed the dozens of workers before us, we talked about a problem over to the schoolhouse.

Chubby Maness had turned into a bully. Chubby never had seemed like the nicest boy in school, but he had recently started pulling some of the girl's pigtails, or tripping some of the smaller boys at recess. When he saw that he was getting away with that, he began hitting boys he was sure he could lick. But Chubby always did his bullying when nobody as big as he was around to straighten him out!

Just this week, Chubby had hit Jackie Cagle in the face, just because Jackie wouldn't give him half of his sweet potato; and he made Earl Junior's nose bleed again. He didn't hit Earl Junior. He just chased him around the playground until Earl Junior's nose started bleeding. Some of us saw what was happening, but, as usual, it was way across the playground from where we was playing.

The first thing that me and Jamie came up with, was that something had to be done to stop Chubby from picking on the littler boys and girls. Then we played catch with a few ideas about what we could and couldn't do:

Telling the teacher or any grown-up was out of the question. It was a matter of honor. You just did not go whining to a grown-up about a problem like Chubby Maness.

It wouldn't do much good to tell Luther Murray neither. One of the things we liked about Luther was his easygoing disposition. He wouldn't let nobody fight in his presence. He was good at putting out fires, but he was not one to rake over the ashes. He sure wasn't about to blow on hot coals to get a fire to blazing again.

We figured that either me or Jamie alone would come out about even with Chubby in a fist fight. We was sure that either of us could swap blow for blow with him, and we was sure that we could take enough punishment to give that bully a lesson. This solution had enough appeal that we was about ready to draw straws for the privilege, when one of us mentioned that what brought this subject up in the first place was the idea of stopping Chubby, not just hurting him. If we had sized him up wrong, he would be even harder to get along with after he had whipped one of us.

Now, you may be thinking that one of us could start something with Chubby and let the other finish him off; or even that we could both jump him together. I'm a little ashamed to admit it, but we did think about it. We didn't seriously consider it, though, because we would then be changing places with Chubby as the bullies. It just wouldn't be right. It might be alright to think about, just after you'd said your prayers for the night – so you could go to sleep with a smile on your face – but you wouldn't want to be a party to such a thing in the real, daylight world.

Whilst we was kicking the problem of Chubby about like a soccer ball, we was all the time watching the insects and robins working the clay in front of us. Without saying nothing about it, we had both noticed that a pair of them robins was carrying the mud to a scrub pine, just about as far away from where we was as the right field is from home plate, over to the baseball park.

Maybe if the robins was making a nest that close, the dirt daubers might be building not too far away, too. We decided to find out.

What we did was not so hard to do as we might have thought. We just followed the flight of one of them daubers, as far as we could keep it in sight, and then waited at that spot until another, or maybe that same dauber came by on another trip. In almost no time, we found that the dirt daubers was building nests in the woodshed.

Then Jamie got an idea. Usually we think of things at about the same time, but this idea belonged to Jamie: if we could follow the dirt daubers from where they got their building material to where they was daubing it, maybe we could find out something about hornets. We had wondered where the hornets got the material for the paper-mache' condominium they was building in one of our pear trees. Perhaps we could follow the hornets from their nest back to the source of their paper. We set about finding out.

Now, one thing you learn pretty quick about hornets is, that you don't want to learn too much about hornets. That is, you want to be very careful just how you set about learning about them. You may learn something from experience that you'd be better off reading about in a book. It might even be better for you to remain ignorant of hornet lore, than to feel the persuasive power of a hornet's argument that it wishes to be left alone. If you ain't ever been stung by a hornet, believe me, folks ain't exaggerating none when they tell you how much they hurt.

We didn't have to get too close to that hornet's nest to see that a lot of the incoming flights was from the direction of the Maness place. Of course, at first, we didn't think of it as the direction of the Maness place. We didn't know how far them hornets was flying, but we didn't think it would be too far.

Honeybees and hornets are alike in one thing besides both having stingers. Once a bee or a hornet knows where he is going, he don't mess around with no sight seeing trips on the way. We found that some of the hornets was chewing up the weathered wood on Old Lady Maness's clothesline posts. We found them as quick and easy as Luther Murray striking out the other side in an inning of baseball.

After we saw what the hornets was doing we wondered why we had never noticed them little tracks in the wood before. A hornet would chew his way along the grain of one of them fence posts a lot like, but faster than, the steam shovel worked its way into a bank of dirt over to the sand pits.

The reason I mention how them hornets was working is because you ought to know they stayed in about the same spot long enough that, if you was brave enough, you might trap one.

Rules of evidence being like they are over to the Yanceyville Courthouse, I might not ought to mention all that me and Jamie considered that day, but since we're talking about Chubby Maness, and the circumstances was unusual, I will mention it.

Hanging on the Maness clothesline was a pair of Chubby's BVDs. We both knowed they was Chubby's, because Old Man Maness wore his long handles all summer long; we had seen them poking out here and there when he sat in the barbers chair over to Mr. Crump's shop. One pair of BVDs on the line this long after the regular Monday morning washday spelled bed-wetting to me and Jamie. I don't say this to slander Chubby, but it bore on the solution to the problem we had both been working on in low gear, while we was watching the hornets and stuff.

The next idea was Jamie's too. It is usually so that I will come up with a good idea pretty soon after Jamie comes up with one, but Jamie was especially keen today.

This is how we sized things up:

Them BVDs wasn't going to be ironed before Chubby put them back on. Old Lady Maness was too busy with other chores, she wasn't going to be ironing BVDs for no bed wetter.

Chubby was likely to put them clean BVDs on after his Saturday night bath.

Here was some hard working Hornets, one of which might be enticed into a change of employment.

This brought up a problem: how do you persuade a hornet to take up a new career, without the persuader being in danger from the hornet. Hornets have been known to raise some powerful objections when somebody set out to change what the hornet was already of a mind to do.

The solution was my idea. What we did was: I hightailed it over to my house to get the bottle of LePages glue which I had left over from making kites, and ran back to where Jamie was still studying on the rest of our problem. It turned out that I had it figgered by this time myself.

We knowed that the Maness family had gone to Danville and would not be likely to get back before dark. Chubby was bragging the day before about all of them going to the carnival and he was expecting to try out every ride. If the family had been at home, we might not have been able to get away with what we did without nobody seeing us.

What we did was: I fetched a long stick and put a big dollop of LePages glue on the small end of it. Then I stationed myself by one of the clothesline posts, and waited for the next hornet to land and start chewing up a load for the trip back to the hornet's nest.

Now, you may find it hard to believe, but it worked on the first hornet I tried it on, and I didn't get stung. Bad as it feels, I was willing to get stung some, if we could finish what we started out to do: but I didn't have to pay that price at all. The big dollop LePages was almost ready to drip off my stick, when I put it on the hornet, so most of it was now on the hornet's back, and it had stopped chewing and was just buzzing and unable to do anything with that load on its back.

Next, we took the BVDs from the line and opened up that slit in the back, that BVDs have for the wearer's convenience, and stuck that hornet inside the BVDs, as smooth as a used car salesman's sales pitch.

We hoped that the hornet would soon stop buzzing, but we looked to see that it was not likely to be discovered when the BVDs was taken in, and we left. In our excitement, we left my glue and the stick I had used, but I ran back to get them. Everything looked normal, with the hornets still working at the clothesline posts, apparently unaware that they were short one worker, which was about to perform a different kind of work, on a different foundation.

Chubby Maness didn't come to Sunday School or Preaching on Sunday. Me and Jamie got together between services and we were pretty sure our plan had worked. We were excited and gleeful about the likelihood of our success. We attempted to hide our smiles behind sober expressions as we went into church and our glee kept us from paying much attention to the order of the service until the preacher announced the text, "Vengeance is Mine, I will repay, 'saith the Lord."

I looked at Jamie and he was looking at me. He had that same expression on his face that Tommy Detwiler had that time when he went into the Ivory Store to claim the prize in the turkey raffle, and found that he had misread one of the digits on his ticket. We was both worried that me and Jamie Klinghopper had undertaken to solve a problem that the Lord has said is His own to solve. It just don't do for us to get impatient that the Lord don't get around to taking care of things, as quick as we want Him to, sometimes. We was feeling pretty low by the time preaching was over.

Me and Jamie didn't get together to play catch or nothing that afternoon. I guess we both wanted to be alone until our hurt started to heal. Reminds me of the time Old Blue got hit with a stray pellet, when the big boys was shooting at a coon. Blue just stayed by hisself, and had the most hurt look on his face, when I went and hugged him and tried to get him to eat something. He was that way until the wound healed. Maybe I thought about Blue now because I was feeling about the same as he did when he was hurt like that and didn't know but what I had had something to do with it.

The thing is, we both knowed that the Lord knowed what we had done. When I tried to say my prayers that night I was bothered that maybe the Lord didn't consider us to be on speaking terms no more. I ain't gonna admit I cried none, but Ma asked me the next morning, if I was feeling alright, so I guess the hurt was showing some.

Chubby Maness came to school Monday morning, and I was about to think that the hornet had rejected his assignment after all, when I noticed that Chubby was not sitting all the way onto the seat of his school desk. When Chubby has only one half of his be-hind on a seat, there is a whole lot of Chubby left hanging over, so I knowed from that, that Chubby couldn't have sat through Sunday School and Preaching the day before.

I guess Chubby was feeling pretty bad, or he wouldn't have told what was bothering him, but he must have told somebody at recess and pretty soon almost everybody was laughing about it, even the teachers at the picnic table.

Everybody seemed to be enjoying Chubby's predicament, except Chubby — and me and Jamie.

Finally, me and Jamie got together to play mumblety peg, and we chewed over some, about what we had done.

Jamie said he had thought a lot about it, and since all we had done was to hurt Chubby, maybe we just ought to stop feeling sorry for ourselves, and finish what we had set out to do. We wasn't really after vengeance. We just wanted to stop Chubby from picking on them little boys and girls. This idea started to brighten things up, like sunshine after a thunderstorm. Before Jamie could finish telling me what he had in mind, Luther Murray rung the bell. Recess was over.

What Jamie did was beautiful, brave, and a big bluff. At afternoon recess, he went to Chubby, where he was standing all alone with his back to a tree, so nobody could tag him on the be-hind. There, he told Chubby exactly what we had done, and why. He also told him that if anybody else found out about this, or he didn't stop picking on the little boys and girls, the next time he might find a copperhead in his socks!

Chubby Maness is a different boy. He don't even chase Earl Junior no more; and he's right much fun to be with, except nobody wants to choose him for their side in baseball, because he can always be throwed out at first base — even if he hits the ball to the outfield.

Now, when I say my prayers, I thank the Lord for how he solved the problem with Chubby Maness.

I want to apologize to you that it took so long to tell about Chubby. I hope you understand that a lot of what we did, didn't take so long as the telling. If listening to me caused you to let a pot boil over, or to miss a bus, or something, I'm sorry. But I did want you to know what me and Jamie had churning in our minds, before bits and pieces began coming together, like butter in Grandma's churn.

I also want to avoid any slander of Chubby. If I left the impression that he wet the bed, please remember that all the evidence we had about that was circumstantial. So, as the judge says, over to the Yanceyville Courthouse, "Strike that, the jury will ignore that remark."

Me and Jamie ain't got no PhD in psychology, but we both got it figured that when the judge says, "Ignore that," the jurors have to ask theirselves, "Ignore what?" and when it's over, some slick lawyer has got that remark as firmly fixed in the minds of them jurors as a cocklebur in a wool sock.

From what we know, you could not prove that Chubby Maness ever wet the bed — that is, you couldn't prove it, over to the Yanceyville Courthouse.

SPRINGHOUSE

If all people all over the world are as glad to get fresh spring water as they are in Caswell County, Pa could soon get to be as rich as Zebulon Fitzwater; except by the time he got the water bottled and sold, it wouldn't be fresh no more. Besides, I can't imagine either Pa or Ma trying to get rich on something they are so glad to give away.

My folks are rightfully proud of the spring, which is the talk of the county, and of the springhouse, which is kept as clean and inviting as an old maid's living room.

The water springs up between two rocks, which look like they might once have been one big rock that split in two. The two great rocks extend beyond the springhouse, so the floor of the springhouse is solid rock, except for where the water runs in and out. The water comes from somewhere deep in the ground and runs out beneath the lattice, as I described before. Pa has filled in a few places with cement, and built a low masonry wall to form a basin for the spring. I guess you can tell that I'm proud of what Pa has done to make this a really nice place to be. The word, "welcome", ain't wrote nowhere on the place, but Pa keeps it painted up real nice; and I heard the mailman say once that the whole place said, "welcome", from a mile away.

Ma keeps a half dozen gourds, which she rotates, so that two gourds are hanging handy at the spring all the time. Nobody who came by, was ever refused a drink, and almost everybody wants a drink, who comes by.

One thing about the springhouse got started before I was born. Just about the first year they was on the place, Pa discovered that one pretty good size spot on the place was ideal for a garden. This spot not only had good deep topsoil, but was in the lea of a huge gray boulder, so that the garden was protected from the winds and on cold nights could draw heat from that boulder, which always drank in heat when the sun was shining.

Pa soon found that he could put out garden plants a good two weeks earlier in his protected garden, than it would be safe to do in other places. I'm not just bragging on my pa, when I report what Ma told me. The reason I'm telling it is to explain how it came to be that Pa almost always has fresh cucumbers, tomatoes, corn and squash before anybody else in the county.

I ain't never yet heard of anybody who raised first rate vegetables that wasn't right proud of what he growed. Since he was first with the best, naturally Pa felt that folks was entitled to see what prize melons, beans, potatoes, and other vegetables he had growed every year. What he did was to put a basket in the springhouse, and put a little note on the basket which said that everything in the basket was for the Baptist preacher. Since the preacher was a frequent visitor to the spring, it followed that this worked out as a great convenience, except that sometimes, for one reason or another, it might have been better to have had a face to face meeting with the preacher.

This idea of Pa's worked out so good for the Baptist preacher, that Mr. Leonard, our neighbor from about a half mile down the road, asked Pa if it would be alright if the Methodists put a basket in the springhouse for their preacher. I've told you about Pa's hospitality. Of course it was alright.

If me and Jamie Klinghopper hadn't done some reading and discussion on the matter, I don't know how I would have tried to express how things developed after them two baskets was put in the springhouse for the two preachers.

Gardeners begin in midwinter to plan their campaigns to outdo each other. Nature holds out on the grower like a virtuous lady and says, "Not yet". Then, one day she surrenders and says, "Take me, I'm yours".

Once the vegetables start coming in, it isn't long before most gardeners have a surplus of something or other that they have planted. Part of the reason is that everybody knows that you should plant a little extra of everything, in case it is a bad season for some crops, so you have what you have planted for insurance, as a surplus. In our county, a whole lot of that surplus came and went through the latticed door of our springhouse.

Pretty soon the preachers was getting more good vegetables to take home than they could rightly use. The lady's circles in the churches was already furnishing plenty of canned good for the preachers' families.

For a while, each of them preachers would find somebody who they was visiting to take some of the extra stuff they had, but it wasn't far into the season when they was almost begging their church members to take some snap beans or something.

One day, when me and Jamie was playing catch under the big poplar trees, both of them preachers came to the springhouse at the same time. Me and Jamie both hollered, "Hi", and kept on trying to sting each other's hands with fast balls.

Pretty soon, we heard the two preachers laughing and talking in the springhouse, like they was as good friends as me and Jamie. We decided it was about time to rest our arms (and stinging left hands) and lay down on our bellies beside the spring branch to watch the thirsty bees and yellow jackets, like we usually did.

Since it was a little after dinner time, the shadows of the tops of them tulip poplars was falling pretty close to where the preachers was having such a good time. So, naturally, we was laying close enough that we could hear what the two men were saying.

This is the joke that got the two men to laughing with each other in the first place: each had a mind to ask the other for help in disposing of some of the good stuff they was obliged to haul off from that springhouse every day. Me and Jamie kind of put that together from the things we heard while we watched the bees and yellow jackets.

"Well, I will approach Brother Friddle on the subject. If he is agreeable, we will meet with you and work this out. I wish all our problems could be no worse than this one". This was from Preacher Ross, the Baptist. "That sounds fine to me. I have certainly enjoyed our little meeting, Brother Ross. I trust that we will have many such meetings in the future". The words of Preacher Ross and Preacher Widenhouse, sure sounded a lot stiffer than the voices me and Jamie heard just before we laid down on our bellies to rest.

Preacher Ross came to see Pa that night after supper, and they met with Preacher Widenhouse the very next afternoon. What they come up with was just about what Jamie and me would have come with, if they would have been of a mind to turn the problem over to us, to chew up and spit out.

Right away, they put a third basket in the springhouse and labeled it, "Community basket – Help yourself".

Preacher Ross announced, in the next service, that the basket had been placed as I described, and he told, also, why it was put there. He praised the people for their "generous contributions of their fine surpluses". He also told about the Methodist preacher making a similar announcement – and the invitation was to the whole community – not just to church people.

There was one other part to the announcement, that sure sounded like it might not work out so good. "If there is a special need, you may put the name of the needy on the basket, and place in the basket a list of the things especially needed".

Then he told us something that made me think that the preacher, or maybe one of the deacons, might be every bit as bright as Jamie. He said that, to start things off, every one of them deacons would put a needy basket in the springhouse, because every one of them deacons had a special need.

Now, me and Jamie ain't been able to figger out why, but no matter how much you may need something, you would like to get what you need, without being called, "needy".

It don't take no PhD in horse sense, to know that everybody who gets help from the welfare department over to Yanceyville, had rather not be called, "needy", just because they are down on their luck. In study period, while Old Lady Showalter is grading papers, she frequently says, "Shush,

I need peace and quiet". Old Lady Showalter don't mean she wants to be called "needy", just because she has a need.

The day after the preachers' announcements, the springhouse looked like somebody was having a basket sale. Me and Jamie went in and read all the little signs and lists. We was reading them list, when Ma came in. She said that she just wanted to greet as many of the people as possible; but she had brought a needy basket with her name on it.

Preacher Ross had put on his basket that he needed more people to turn out on visitation nights. As soon as Ma had read the preachers list, she went out to the road where the preacher was throwing baseball a few times with Earl Junior. Of course the preacher stopped to talk to Ma. Pretty soon after they said whatever they said, Preacher Ross came in and replaced his list: it read now, "A black necktie".

When I saw what was wrote on the preacher's new list, I felt like I knowed, all of a sudden, who it was among grown-ups who, when it came to smarts, didn't have to take a back seat to Jamie Klinghopper.

Ma's idea seems to have worked very well. The activity down at the springhouse got back to near normal in a couple of days. The bees and yellow jackets appeared to be glad of it.

Me and Jamie don't feel like we yet understand what makes people do what they do sometimes. But the way we've got it figgered up to now is that, although pride has something to do with folks taking their very best vegetables and things to give away, maybe part of it is a kind of thanksgiving and praise to the "One Who Gives" these fine things, in the first place.

Anyways, it don't seem to be hurting people's pride none, when they put a needy basket in the springhouse, saying they need a baby blanket, or booties, or something.

There has been a side effect to the basket program that me and Jamie, and maybe Ma or the preachers or deacons, didn't think about. The exchange of vegetables is working so well that the truck farmers have to go all the way over to Yanceyville, or to Danville, to sell their stuff. Pickard's Grocery and the Ivory Store don't have no vegetable market no more.

You're probably thinking that what I've told you is too good to be true, and if I left it like this, you would be right.

The springhouse was cleaned out by thieves only two times last year. We like to think that the pillagers was from somewhere outside the county. Me and Jamie chewed over what we would like to do to the ones who would spoil such a good setup. We even considered using some oil of pepper to set up a trap to straighten the thieves out. Then we remembered the incident with Chubby Maness.

I must have said something to Ma about what was brewing in mine and Jamie's heads, because she said, just before I went to my room for the night, "Frankie, whoever it was who took everything from the springhouse, just might have needed it. Wasn't it put there for that?"

When I said my prayers, I thanked the Lord for a ma who was so smart as my ma — and so loving.

BILL AND HARVEY

Ma agreed to help me and Jamie. Leastways, that's the way I remember it. It might be that she made the suggestion in the first place. One of the really great things about my ma is that whenever you do something that pleases her, she makes you feel like things are your idea, even if she guided you into it.

It's hard to talk to grown-ups about important things like hating something the preacher said. It ain't no trouble at all to say just about anything that comes into my head to Jamie Klinghopper. Maybe it's because with grown-ups you are afraid you won't measure up to the standard they've set for you, and you don't want to disappoint them by letting them see how stupid you can be. You especially don't want them to know that you can be sinful. With Jamie, talk is easy, because there ain't nothing one of us is guilty of, without the other being just as guilty. If we're not guilty about exactly the same things, we're as guilty about something similar; so the problem of judging each other just never comes up.

As far as saying stupid things, we sometimes seem to try to outdo each other in stupidity; but we just have a good laugh about it, and go on. It seems like the more stupid things we say and do together, the more we learn about life.

Anyways, I know I didn't exactly tell Ma that me and Jamie Klinghopper was worried about the fellers over at Thacker's Boarding House, "going to hell in a hand-basket", when maybe me and Jamie could do something about it. You just don't say things like that to your ma. I suspicion that she got the idea, though, because by the time I got with Jamie to work out the details, it seemed like a whole lot of it was already settled.

What me and Jamie did was to go over to Thacker's Boarding House just as they were finished with their pork chops, creasy greens, candied yams, cornbread, and all; and invited a couple of them over to my house for Saturday supper. I guess we didn't think it through too good, or we might have thought of a better time to ask them. The fellers we asked, had just sat down in the parlor to write letters home. It turned out to be easy.

I guess Ma was a lot smarter than I thought. It was her who figgered that whoever we invited would be coming from the harvest fields, all dirty and sweaty; and they might be as interested in swimming and fishing and family entertainment, as in facing uncertain chances for dates on Saturday night.

So our invitation was for sandwiches and cold chicken, at Mabry's Mill, where we would be fishing; to be followed by an evening with my folks. We explained that we would spend some time there at the pond, where they could swim and fish with us until about four o'clock. Then, if our luck was good, me and Jamie would high tail it home to clean and dress the fish, while the two men went for their regular visit to the barbershop, and to the boarding house to change clothes. Ma wouldn't drop the fish in the pan until the fellers got to our house (we figgered about six-thirty). We even had a back-up of country ham, roasting ears, and such, if the fish was not biting.

It worked beautiful.

When we got to Mabry's Mill that Saturday, I had a kind of lump in my throat and a feeling in my chest, like you have when you hit one of Luther Murray's fast balls. Jamie must have felt about the same. We had started to feel a little anxious, though, when it was almost time for the fellers to come and we hadn't caught anything. Jamie mentioned about how, in the Bible, the fishermen had toiled all night and caught nothing. This made me hope for a great draught of fishes.

The fish had started biting by the time our guests had taken a quick dip under the water wheel. Ma had been sure that we had brought some clean drinking water and a bucket of clean water so we could all wash our hands before eating the picnic lunch. These were hard working men, but it was fun to hear them laughing and talking together, as if this was every bit as much fun for them as we had hoped it would be.

When we had finished our picnic, we all fished some, and we began to fill up our lines with good fish, even including some largemouth bass. While it wasn't exactly a miraculous catch, we had plenty for our supper a good half-hour before we had expected to quit fishing. Bill, the older of the two, told us how we could gig for frogs in the pond, and a whole lot of other things I can't remember just now.

Bill and Harvey offered to help us clean the fish, but we told them we could handle it. I think this was maybe the biggest catch we ever had, though, and we were a little anxious about the time.

We needn't have worried. Pa was there, ready to help us, when we got home. Everything that could be made ready ahead of time was done; and we all had the fish cleaned and dressed by the time H.V. Kaltenborn came on the radio.

We had a lot of fun that night. Besides putting away the best fish supper this county ever got wind of, we had each other's company. Ma was good at the piano, and Pa had a good bass voice. We sung a lot of happy songs, and laughed and talked until about nine o'clock, when Ma served the apple and cherry pies. Bill and Harvey, and Ma and Pa, all had coffee. Me and Jamie each had a tall glass of cool sweet milk. I really believe that we all had a good time. Bill and Harvey gave as good as they got, when it came to family entertainment.

Ma offered to put Bill and Harvey up for the night, so they could go to church with us the next day. We really didn't expect them to stay, since their rooms was already paid for, over to Thacker's Boarding House. They said that they would see us in church next morning. Bill said he wanted to hear Pa's voice, singing them hymns.

We said goodnight pretty early. Bill and Harvey said they would walk Jamie home. I guess they did walk Jamie home, but they needn't have bothered. Jamie might be scared of haunted houses, and maybe a little skittery about walking past a graveyard late at night, but he sure ain't scared to walk from my house to his, on a Saturday night when the moon is out.

We got kind of tied up in Sunday School; with Davie Snodgrass wanting to know just how big was Goliath; and how many rocks little David had picked up for his slingshot; and how did he make a slingshot without no automobile inner tubes. So we didn't get to see if Bill and Harvey had really come to preaching service, like they said they would.

Ma and Pa don't make me sit in front of them no more, like they did when I was a little shaver – so's Ma could see that I bowed my head for prayers, and I didn't push my knee into Shirley Holliday's fat fanny, when she sat too close. I can sit just about anywheres in the church I want to now; but boy! I better be in there somewhere – and be behaving myself.

Well, this was one time when I wanted to sit with my family. There was Bill and Harvey, already seated in the pew right behind Ma and Pa. It made me feel so good to see them that I felt almost like I did when Gladys Riddle sent me that valentine.

Jamie Klinghopper slipped in beside Bill and Harvey, and I sat beside Ma and Pa. We had just finished shaking hands all around, like we was all grown-ups, when the opening hymn was announced by Hobert Hinshaw.

Well! That preacher might have slept late on some mornings, like I thought, but when he got started that morning, he sure sounded a whole lot more convincing to me. He wasn't just raking them hard working harvest fellers over the coals this time. He gave us all a raking over, and included hisself in the sorry mix with the rest. Either the preacher hisself had just got religion, or I was hearing him different; because he made it plain that no group of people was any better than any others, and that we was all under the wrath of God. I tell you it was scary!

After the preacher had made it plain that we was all in so much trouble with God, that we could never dig our way out, he began to tell us what God had done to get us out. I believe I understood about grace more after hearing that sermon. And I wasn't mad at the preacher anymore.

We all sounded good singing them hymns. I noticed that our pew was getting a lot of attention, and I thought it was because of Pa's bass and our voices blended in – until I realized that the admiring glances was coming from the young women in the congregation, who always looked that way

48

at men as handsome as Bill and Harvey. I felt rather sorry for the preacher, when nobody went down front at the invitation; even after we had sung two extra verses of, "Just As I Am".

After service, Ma and Pa introduced Bill and Harvey to the other folks. The Snodgrass family invited Bill and Harvey to their house for the next Saturday afternoon and evening. Several church members invited our visitors to dinner, but they said, "No thanks, we're expected at Mrs. Thacker's".

The next week, we did almost the same thing, except it was with two other fellers, and it was at Jamie Klinghopper's house where we ate the fish.

Soon Ma's circle made it a point to see that somebody in the circle had a special supper every Saturday night while the harvest crews was in town, and invited some of them young men to supper.

Like I said, I don't come right out and tell Ma some of the things that bother me. Me and Jamie had talked over our disappointment that Bill and Harvey hadn't gone down and took the preacher's hand, after such a good sermon. We was kind of puzzled that so much of our plan had gone so well – even better than we had dared to hope as far as new friendships – and we couldn't see that it had really done any good at all. I must have said enough to Ma that she understood what was tumbling over in my mind; because she said, "Don't worry, Frankie. You did what you could. God doesn't ask for more".

After Ma said what she did, and I saw that Bill and Harvey was coming to church the other two Sundays they was in town, I felt some better.

Jamie Klinghopper said, "We might not have kept anybody from "going to hell in a hand-basket", but I believe we sure put a hole in that hand-basket".

I told you Jamie was smart.

TRAMPS

One day that summer, two tramps came down the road and stopped at the springhouse for a drink. Ma says you shouldn't judge folks by their appearance, but I knowed them fellers was tramps: by the look of the dust on their blue denims, you could see that they had tramped a long way.

Well, tramps can get as thirsty as anybody, so it didn't bother me none that they would get a cool drink. I did think, though, about how somebody had taken everything from all the baskets a couple of times, so I left off chopping stove wood as soon as I saw that the two men, coming down the road from town, was strangers. I thought this was a good time to fetch in the milk and butter for supper.

The two fellers was already in the springhouse when I got down to the grove of poplars. There was two knapsacks just outside the door, on the little bench that Pa had put there just after the needy baskets was started. (Pa had also put a picnic table under the oak trees, so folks could socialize in better comfort – what with the benches and all).

When I walked into the springhouse, each of the men had a gourd full of spring water up to his face, like he couldn't hardly wait to taste it. I waited until they had finished gulping down that water before I said, "Hi". (Folks in our county always speak when they meet somebody, even if it ain't in their own springhouse). They both said, "Hello", and went right back to drinking the water.

I went on over to the little shelf that Pa had fixed so the cold water would flow around the bottles and jars and the jars wouldn't get too far down into the stream. I wasn't in no hurry to finish with the chore I'd

51

selected to perform at this time, but I didn't want to be so slow that them fellers would guess that I was really there to see that they didn't mess up nothing.

One of the men said, "So you live here?"

They say that in the Chinese languages, voice inflection can cause a word to have an entirely different meaning than the same word, spoken in a different way. It is easy to believe it is so, when you think about how the words spoken in English can sometimes be either a statement or a question, depending on how it is said. This man had just asked a question, but he asked it like he knew the answer would be positive. Of course I realized right away that he had to know that I either lived there, or I was about to steal something from them jars.

After I had told them my name and they had told me theirs, they started asking questions about the springhouse and the needy baskets and all. It was plain to me, right away, that they had already heard a lot about the springhouse from what others had told them.

It would have been awkward to explain about the use of the needy baskets without inviting the men to help themselves from the community basket. After I had told them that they should take what they wanted, I felt a little guilty that I had found it hard to say. They each took a tomato and a couple of early summer apples that somebody had left there, and they was both looking real interested in a watermelon.

I told them that they could use the picnic table and cut the melon right there if they wanted to. It turned out that they wanted to.

I took the milk and butter on up to the house while the men was eating the watermelon. Naturally, Ma wanted to know why I was bringing them in so early. I told her about the tramps.

I declare! Sometimes Ma can be just about as easy to talk to as Jamie. She seemed to understand, right away, that I was a little uneasy about them fellers down there right now. They was bound to be making a mess of watermelon rinds and seeds for me to clean up, so the yellow jackets don't take over the place. She told me that part in the Bible about entertaining angels unawares.

I went back to talk to the two men some more before they moved on, and before it was time for me to go to supper.

They had obviously enjoyed the melon, and I had a whole lot less to do to clean up than I had expected. They continued to ask questions about the people in the county, and especially about the springhouse.

Just about the time the sun got low enough to shine on about half the springhouse, one of them fellers got out a camera from his knapsack, and starting taking pictures of the house.

When I asked them about how they happened to have a camera, they explained that they were on vacation from the University of Chicago, and they were hiking through some parts of the South to do a book on, "Americana", they called it. They had heard about the springhouse from somebody who had stayed for a while at Thacker's Boarding House, and they had come by this way to make it part of their story.

The man with the camera said that, so far, the springhouse was the most likely subject for the book's cover.

Before they left, one of them gave me a present for Ma. While they was at the picnic table, he had wrote a poem about "The Spirit Behind the Springhouse", special for my ma.

I know it would be a big thrill to think about entertaining angels from Heaven, unawares; but to be aware that you've entertained poets from the University of Chicago – that ain't so bad either.

I realize I never told you the names of them two tramps with doctor's degrees from the University of Chicago. I hope you will please excuse me for that. If I told you their names, you might think I was trying to get you to go out and buy a book with the picture of our springhouse on the cover, and I don't want that. Besides, the book ain't out yet. I know, because every time I go over to Danville, I go into the bookstore to ask about it.

Pa has made a nice frame for Ma's poem. He put it in a waterproof case which he made just for the poem. He has it mounted just over the spring so everybody who wants to can read it. It is in the author's own handwriting, signed and everything. Ma is proud to have the poem, but she won't make too much over it. I know her!

SPRINGHOUSE

All passersby who tarry here
To taste the nectar from this spring,
Are reflected in the water clear,
As they take the Earth's sweet offering.

Take what you need, my needy friend,
And give the bounty you can spare.

Give of free spirit, to this end
This house is made a place to share.

And see reflected in this pool
The image of a happy face;
For you have set the spirit rule
That makes this a refreshing place.

DUCK POND

This here happened a long time ago.

Me and Jamie was messing around behind Old Man Peabody's tobacco barn, trying to get some doodlebugs to come out of their holes, when Jamie said he had to go use the outhouse. Now Jamie didn't really say, "I have to go use the outhouse." The reason I said he had to go use the outhouse is because Ma said that is what you should say when you want to do what Jamie wanted to do.

Now, wait! If I leave it like that, you'll maybe think that Jamie said something he didn't say, and I don't want you to think that Jamie would say things like that. What Jamie said sounds like the letter that follows the letter "o" in the alphabet, and it sounds like the name of a little green vegetable that comes in a pod, but you don't want to say them sounds when you're talking about what Jamie wanted to do. I didn't say that what Jamie was about to do sounds like that; what he said, sounds like that. What Jamie wanted to do sounds like when the first few gravels fall as the tailgate of a dump truck opens.

Well, let's get back to Jamie, before he wets his pants. Now, why didn't I think of that sooner? That's what Jamie wanted to do – except not in his pants!

I said, "Well, Jamie, why don't you just go over behind that tobacco sled between them blackjack oaks?" Jamie was lookin' kind of anxious, but he was cautious, "Old Man Peabody might come by where he will see what I done before it dries."

Jamie was looking desperate, so I said, "Let's try the door of the tobacco barn and see if we can get inside." But the preacher says, 'Do unto others as you would have them do unto you', and I sure wouldn't want anybody doing unto me like that." That Jamie had character alright, but by now he also had a pretty full bladder.

I told Jamie that if he would just try to hold out, I would walk with him over to use Old Man Peabody's outhouse. I guess Jamie was afraid to even speak now because he just started heading around the duck pond towards the little path that runs from Old Man Peabody's back door, by the duck pond, to the Peabody comfort station.

Well, me and Jamie wasn't to be very lucky on this day, because before we was hardly started down the path, the door to the outhouse opened and out stepped Mrs. Peabody with Shirley, her little girl.

It was too late to run the other way, and Jamie probably couldn't have anyhow, so we kept moving, at a walk, toward the pair that was walking back towards the Peabody house.

Just as we got close enough for Mrs. Peabody to call, "Why, hello, Jamie, Howdy, Frankie," I saw the circle starting on Jamie's overalls.

You may find what I did inexcusable, but I didn't know nothing else to do. This was one time we couldn't talk over what to do next. Jamie was my friend – I pushed him into the duck pond!

Jamie was too shocked at what he had done to hardly notice what I did to get him out of the embarrassment. "Pretend we're mad", I said, as Mrs. Peabody rushed up to stop the fight she saw going on in front of her.

We didn't really hit each other. Jamie yelled, "I'm gonna tell your Ma."

He sounded like he was mad, but he had the most relieved look on his face that he'd had since we was calling them doodlebugs: Come out, come out, wherever you are, doodlebug, doodlebug, your house is on fire." We never told the truth to them doodlebugs but we never lied about Jamie's pants being wet.

I just took a lickin' for pushing Jamie into the duck pond. But it just couldn't be helped. Jamie was my friend.

Pa delivers the lickin's at my house. It may seem awful old fashioned to have such a division of labor, but at our house, some things was man's work – some things was woman's work A good lickin' was considered a man's job.

Ma did the interrogatin'. Old Lady Peabody had done her Christian duty by telling Ma that she saw me shove Jamie into the duck pond. Mrs. Peabody took care of the how: by a shove to Jamie's shoulders; what: I had pushed him into the pond; when: that afternoon when the shadows of the hickory trees had just struck the privy; where: on the privy path and in the duck pond.

Why – was a lot harder. Ma kept after me, "But, why, Frankie? You and Jamie are such good friends! But why can't you say, Frankie?" Ma really wanted to know.

Now, a lot of folks can't understand this, but it didn't take long for Ma to find out that I just wasn't going to tell her why. Ma said, "Frankie, since you and Jamie are getting along alright now, I'm not going to insist that you tell me anymore. But remember, when your father gets home, you will be punished for pushing Jamie into the duck pond."

I don't tell lies to my parents, maybe it's because I've learned that they fully expect me to tell the truth, and will respect my wish not to tell private things. I believe Ma guessed that I was protectin' Jamie. I don't believe she guessed, from what. Pa gave me the lickin'. I won't describe it to you except to say that he made sure I got his message. But Pa is not a cruel man. The lickin' was for my learnin', not for Pa's enjoyment. I knowed that Ma and Pa both hated to see me get a lickin'.

Since I knowed that Pa wasn't really mad at me, and because it was for my friend, it didn't hurt hardly at all.

I still don't know why it seemed so important to me not to tell Ma about what Jamie had done in his pants and in the duck pond. It would have been difficult, but I could have told her if it had been me that couldn't hold his water.

I guess I didn't want Jamie to have any reason to be embarrassed before my ma, and I didn't want Ma to see any weakness in my friend, Jamie.

I've thought about it some, and I think I might know part of the why of this: a whole lot of struggling we have to do in life is for control. Over to the baseball park, them pitchers are all the time practicing pitching them baseballs over the plate, to anybody they can get to catch for them, so they can get enough control over their fast balls, curves, and drops, to get the ball to go where they intend. A good pitcher is proud of his control of the strike zone.

It just didn't seem fittin' for Ma to know that Jamie had temporarily lost control of something he had kept pretty well in harness since he was two years old.

59

If grown-ups didn't get into no more trouble over loss of control, than me and Jamie did at Old Man Peabody's duck pond, then I reckon there'd be a whole lot less trouble in the world.

SPECIAL CHILD

Shirley Peabody is a special child. Once, I heard the old biddies in Ma's circle talking, and they said that "special child" is a euphemism for "retarded". I ain't even going to call the name of the old biddy that said it, but I looked it up (that's why it's spelled right), and I guess she may be partly right. The thing is, it don't make me, nor nobody else that's worth a hoot, think nothing less of Shirley. She is a special child.

You may already have guessed that Shirley is special, by her ma going to the outhouse with her. I guess there may be two reasons why her ma goes with Shirley: one is that Shirley really does need help with most things, and the other is that she is so loving that her ma just wants to be with her as much as she can. Shirley is as loving to be around as a warm puppy – but you need to be extra careful not to run into her when you are chasing one of Old Man McElwaine's goats through the Peabody yard, or herding your guinea hens back to the pen. Shirley could dodge you all right except that she never seems to notice that she should get out of the way.

Mrs. Peabody used to run out and take Shirley into the house when she knew that some animal was loose or something that might mean folks would be running in her yard. Mrs. Peabody found out that me and Jamie feel almost as protective of Shirley as she does. Now, she ain't so quick to run out and grab her.

Snow came early last year. It ain't so unusual for us to get some snow flurries that early, but I'm talking about a snow that would make a rabbit glad to have fur all around. (It's like having fur lined underwear with the flap up.)

The snow started to fall in tiny, almost unnoticed little bits Ma said was called "hominy". The sky had been solid overcast all day, and it grew heavier as the day was about to call it quits.

I was on my way back to the house with water and buttermilk from the springhouse, when I first noticed that them little bits of snow was falling, as softly as old Tom walks when he's stalking a field mouse. I caught some of them little bits of fluff on my arms, as much as I could with my arms akimbo, what with a load in each hand. Before I could get them into the house to show Ma, they was already melted.

There is something about snow that kind of gets your pepper up. Pas was almost as excited as me and Ma was; as we hurried with supper so me and Pa could bring in extra firewood for the fireplace and range, in case it snowed heavy.

By the time we had finished with our meal and walked to the woodpile, them little hominy snowflakes was falling right steady, and we left tracks in the white that was covering the path. When we had finished loading the porch with all the firewood it would hold, the whole ground was white and the flakes was getting bigger.

Ma was at the door watching when we finished. She had cleaned up the dishes and put them away, and stood there in the doorway with excitement in her face and love in her eyes, for me and for Pa, and for the sight of the snowflakes a'falling. We all regretted that the daylight was fading too fast for us to see for very long the flakes of snow, as big now as goose feathers.

It probably could not be true in the sections of the nation where snow comes more often, but when it snows in our part of the country, it is rare enough that it seems that love descends with the snow and covers the Earth like a blanket. The feeling I had is hard to describe. I guess it was, on the outside, like the still water in the pool over to the rock quarry, but inside, there was an undertow of excitement. We went into the living room, where the piano and the big fireplace are. Ma played some happy songs on the piano. We all sang some and then popped some corn at the fireplace.

Pa went outside two or three times to see if it had snowed enough to fetch some in for snow cream. We gave it up about half past eight o'clock. Ma brewed some hot cocoa and made some caramel to coat some of our popcorn. It was a long way past just nice.

We had a devotional before bedtime. We didn't do this every night, but it wasn't unusual. I don't think I've ever felt more secure in my life. With my ma and pa and me sharing hot cocoa, popcorn, peanuts and prayers, and with the Lord sending down all of them little white love notes from Heaven, I didn't have a worry in the world.

NEIGHBORS

It stopped snowing a little after daylight next morning, with about seven inches of snow on the ground. No school today!

The whole countryside was as though it was covered with a wedding dress of white, and it was virgin pure. Still we knowed that down at the cow lot and in the pigpens; in fact, everyplace, it was not so pure as it looked with seven inches of snow covering the filth.

Ma mentioned at breakfast that she was a little concerned about the Peabody household. "I don't see any smoke coming from the big chimney over at the Peabody place this morning. There is a little smoke coming from the range flue, but something must be wrong."

We studied in school about them American Indians being able to pick up clues about travelers and all; but my ma could pick up signs and clues on so little evidence that they would have had Sherlock Holmes asking Doctor Watson for advice. Of course, this was one of the simple ones, because, living where we did, with so few houses around, your eye would just naturally pick up things like smoke coming from one chimney and not another.

On the night before, we had all three seen that there was a big plume of smoke rising from the great fireplace at the Peabody's. I remembered that I'd seen the big chimney smoking at Mr. Leonard's. I didn't remember about the small flue, but it wasn't unusual for the Leonard's to let the fire die out in the kitchen range after an early supper.

After breakfast, I went into the closed up (and cold) front room, where I could see the Peabody place better. I figgered that, with the snow and all, Mr. Peabody was just burning the dry wood from where it had been stored on his porch, and it wasn't giving out no smoke. The air looked calm over the chimney. If there had been a hot fire in the fireplace, there might not have been smoke, but there would have been other evidence. You know them little wavery lines you see when heat rises through the air; like you ain't looking straight at what it looks like you're looking straight at. Anything behind that heat looks like it keeps jumping about.

Anyways, I could tell that Ma was right. From where I was I could see the back of the Peabody place, the privy and all. I remembered all at once, about seeing Mrs. Peabody and Shirley coming from the privy and I got really worried. There wasn't no sign that anybody had been to the privy. What if Mrs. Peabody takes Shirley in her arms and starts to the privy; and what if, on the way they slip and fall into the duck pond, and little Shirley falls into deep water. For somebody who didn't have a worry in the world last night, I was thinking of a lot of "what-ifs", all of a sudden.

I hadn't been in no special hurry up to now. I already had on my high top boots that was nearly new that I got from the Shanks boy, who had outgrowed them last year. I was looking forward to getting out and making them treaded tracks that nearly new boots leave in the snow and mud.

Ma said, "Frankie, wrap up good and go over to the Peabody place and see if there is anything they need. "Alright, Ma", I answered right away, but I didn't leave right away. I waited for the next line: "And take Mrs. Peabody this pound cake I have wrapped for her."

Pa had been out before it even stopped snowing, and cleaned a path to our privy. Other places we had to go could be tramped through in our high top boots, but Ma didn't need to wade through no seven inch snow to get to the outhouse; Pa saw to that, and early.

Seven inches of snow was more than I had ever walked through before. You have two choices, when the snow was as soft as this was: you can pick up your feet, out of their tracks, or you can push right through the snow. Either choice you make is fun when you start, but it becomes tiring. I don't mean you get bored. I mean you get tired. By the time I got to Mrs. Peabody's with the slices of pound cake Ma had sent, I was tuckered.

Mrs. Peabody looked a little tuckered herself, when she came to the door. The first thing she did was to say, "Come on in out of the cold, Frankie. You'll catch cold standing there like that." Mas are a lot alike in wanting to see to your comfort before they begin considering any problems they might have. "Warm yourself in here by the kitchen range with Shirley. Mr. Peabody was sick all night, and I haven't got a fire started in the fireplace yet." "Ma sent you this," I said, as I handed her the little package, which was wrapped in *Cut-Rite* wax paper. "Thank you, Frankie, and thank your mother for me, and have a seat," was what she said, all the time pulling at my wraps and things, the way mas do.

"Ma sent me over to see was it anything you needed, Mrs. Peabody, and I wondered if I could clean a path to the privy for you, and maybe get your fire to going," the words kind of spilled out of me.

While I was resisting Mrs. Peabody trying to pull my coat off, I noticed that there was a few spots of water on the linoleum, like somebody had been outside and tracked snow into the kitchen. I thought maybe Mr. or Mrs. Peabody had been outside since I had checked the privy path from our window.

"That's kind of you, Frankie, but Slim Jackson is out there this very minute with Mr. Peabody's shovel, working on that path. I'll accept your offer to start a fire in the big fireplace, though. It's really cold in the bedroom where Mr. Peabody is, and a fire would sure be a help." Mrs. Peabody don't usually say that many words in a row, and I guessed she was trying to cover up her concern about how things were going to work out for her husband. It's kind of like whistling when you walk past the graveyard at night when the moon ain't shinin'.

It didn't take hardly no time for me to get the fire going. There was good dry wood and light'ard knots that Mr. Peabody had laid out ready.

I asked Mrs. Peabody was there anything more I could do in the house. When she said not I asked, "Is there anything you want Ma or Pa to do for you?" She answered that maybe Pa could go for Dr. Spoon if Mr. Peabody's fever didn't come down soon. "And I could use some help with the milking and gathering the eggs. I'll just put some feed out at the back door for the ducks and chickens, if you'll just clear a little spot there near the house."

When I went out the back door, I saw Slim Jackson for the first time that morning. He was the oldest of Aunt Lucy's children, who lived about a quarter of a mile across the fields from the back of the Peabody place. Aunt Lucy, or one of her children sometimes take care of Shirley when Mrs. Peabody has to be away for some reason, which isn't often.

Slim turned and said, "Hi", when he heard the door close. He had already cleared a neat path about two thirds of the way to the privy. After answering, "Hi" back to Slim, I went out to where he was moving the snow and asked if I couldn't spell him for awhile. He said, "Thanks, but I'll get cold if I ain't moving." He was sweating right good when he said that so I said, "Let me shovel until you begin to feel chilly, then we'll trade off." "That sounds good," was what he said.

I took the pointed shovel, which was probably the only kind Mr. Peabody had. Nobody much in our part of the country has to shovel snow often. Even with the seven inches of snow, the shovel never was heavy, but it took a lot of scoops to make much progress. It was still kind of fun.

I told Slim about what I'd seen from my window, about what Ma had said, and asked him how he came to be there, helping Mrs. Peabody. Would you believe that his Ma had made the same kind of Sherlock Holmes deductions as my Ma; and they were concerned for Shirley, just like me.

When I thought about it later, it shamed me some that Slim had got to the Peabody house before me. The Jacksons didn't go to the same church, or to the same school, but they had been the first to respond to the need they had surmised was at the Peabody's'.

Me and Slim worked together to get enough firewood in, to clear that place for the ducks and chickens and in gathering the chicken and duck eggs. It was fun working and talking with Slim, and I admired the way he went about getting things done. He soon left, though, to report to his ma what he had learned; and I went home to tell mine. I was near tuckered again when I got to the house. I was feeling good about helping, but I was still kind of anxious.

Pa was back in the house when I got back with my report. He put his boots back on in a hurry and headed over to milk the cow for Mrs. Peabody.

When Pa got back, it was to tell us that he was going, straight away, to see if he could fetch Dr. Spoon. Ma and I ate dinner alone, and we were not as happy as we had been the night before.

It's funny how we take life, and even good health for granted. If we didn't know it already, the preacher tells us that we are going to die. We don't disbelieve the preacher but mostly we go on about our business like it wasn't so at all that we was going to die. In our prayers we thank the Lord for good health; but it seems like the healthier we are the more likely we are to take it for granted. We don't exactly expect to live forever – just today and tomorrow and the day after; and we keep on expecting that until what we don't expect, comes.

Pa brought Dr. Spoon back in his "A" model. His car traveled better in the snow than the doctors'. The doctor did what he could. Mr. Peabody was too far gone with pneumonia when Doctor Spoon got there. Mr. Peabody died the next morning.

By the time of nightfall on the day that the snow finished falling, over half of it had melted away. Since it melts mostly from underneath, it kind of surprises you that its not so deep anymore and pretty soon it reminds you of a fallen soufflé. But the ground was still white, most all around when we had a very quiet supper. We sang no songs that night but we did have prayer together.

Pa went to check on Mr. Peabody the first thing the next morning, the morning of Mr. Peabody's death, and then came back to fetch Ma right away. It was one of the few mornings I ever woke up and didn't smell breakfast cooking in the kitchen. Of course, it was no trouble for me to figger where my folks were. I put on my clothes as quick as I could and went over there. The undertaker was just taking Mr. Peabody's remains away when I got there. That is not the best way to learn that a neighbor has died.

I didn't even go inside. I turned around, went home, and cried. I didn't cry just because it was appropriate to the occasion, but I cried, and I didn't even understand why I was crying. I did know some of the things that might be bothering me: I was hungry; I cried for Shirley, who had lost her Pa; I cried for Mrs. Peabody, who lost a good husband; I cried for Ma and Pa who had lost a good neighbor; and I cried for me, because I really didn't understand why I was crying. I couldn't understand why the Lord let me be so happy on one night and so full of tears this soon after. I cried because I was crying when I should be out doing something about the needs of Mrs. Peabody and Shirley, whose was the real loss.

I cried in anger for my tears; and I didn't want anybody to see me crying.

Finally the tears ceased – but not the sorrow. All of a sudden I thought I understood how Old Blue must have felt when he was hurt and I couldn't console him with my hugs and caring.

When the snubbing had ended, I still didn't fully understand my tears.

LITERATURE APPRECIATION

Old Lady Showalter said that we would study this year about literature. I don't think she means that we will study anything like "Smiling Jack", or The Katzenjammer Kids". She said we would study about a long feller, and maybe we would get to Milton.

I like literature. The reason I like it is probably because when we have literature, Old Lady Showalter reads to us. Boy, is this something different! The teacher doesn't seem like a old lady at all when she reads, and she has a really comfortable way of saying the words that make you feel like you're taking a long trip somewhere with a beautiful lady for company. And you can let your mind draw pictures as she reads.

Like the time I got a quick picture of Zeb's winter underwear hanging in the sunshine on the Crookshank clothes line, when she read about long johns, silver. I remember the mental image of a very long cat, when she read "A Tale of Two Cities". I see colored eggs on Easter Island: things like that. I figger my mind will be able to draw some good pictures when she reads about "Long Feller".

Now I don't know why we might take a field trip to Milton. Milton ain't very far and there ain't nothing there that I know of, except maybe some old houses and the general store. But, any field trip at all will be exciting.

Teacher says that we will study literature appreciation. Well, that's fine with me, but I already appreciate literature, like I said. Old Lady Showalter seems like she has changed into a warm young woman, when she reads to us.

Tomorrow all of us are supposed to bring to school anything we like to read, so that we can see what literature appreciation is all about. She at first said that we could recite any poem that we chose, whether it was considered literature or not, so long as we liked it; but when Jamie mentioned a limerick about a man from Nantucket, she changed her mind. She said she was glad that Jamie appreciated the limerick, but it would be best if she read our selections before they are recited to the class.

I found out that one of my favorites is by somebody that ain't in any of the schoolbooks. I got all the more in the notion that it was my favorite, when Gladys said that she was going to talk about a rhyme by the same man.

This sounded like the kind of chance I was waiting for, so I asked if I could come over to her house after school and we could do our homework together. She said it would be alright!

Boy, I ain't never been so excited about anything in my life! I was going to get to talk to Gladys without Jamie Klinghopper or any of the other boys around – just me and her, gee!

When I got over to Gladys' house, I was kind of nervous, but Mrs. Riddle came to the front door and said I should come on in. Gladys and me could do our homework in the front parlor, while her mother was fixing supper in the kitchen.

I took a seat and Gladys came in.

Alone with Gladys at last!

We picked up right where we left off at school about her and me choosing rhymes by the same unknown. It didn't seem so strange when we realized they were by Freddie Glover's grandfather. Freddie had been pushing those rhymes on us for about a year, but we like some of them.

I told Gladys I would show her mine, if she would show me hers. She giggled and said, "Alright". But she checked to be sure that her mother was still busy in the kitchen.

I don't want to sound disappointed or anything, but hers wasn't much more than a simple line, while mine was long and hard.

Well, anyhow, I was still alone with Gladys, and even if the sentence she showed me was such a simple thing, I felt like I was flying in the clouds: I was alone with a special girl, while her mother was busy fixing supper in the kitchen.

My rhyme was, "Mae West".

I won't tell you what Gladys' was, that's her report.

Mae West

We like to see Mae West perform.

Her act is never just the norm:

When she's on stage,

Our gazes graze

The outlines of a perfect form.

She is certainly well developed.

Her minuses must be few,

And all of them kept enveloped

In the pluses that we view.

When I accepted her warm invitation
To "Come up and see me some time",
I went with high expectation,

For she is a dish that is prime.
I had hoped to get down to basics,
But she entertained with her wit.
When I protested her tactics,

She wasn't bothered a bit.
When she'd said I should come up and see her,
She was merely throwing a curve:
Her ample chest was offered only in jest.

To think otherwise, "really took nerve".
She boxed my face for my efforts.
I was shocked at the turn of events.
Her staggers and smiles

Are but part of her wiles.
They're made without vulgar intent.
But the lady is really no boxer.
If she were, she would probably win:

A clever foe might outfox her,
But she never leads with her chin.

The lines she delivers are clever,
But easily misunderstood.

She's good in the way she delivers,
But she never delivers the goods.

"C"

I got a "C" on my report on "Mae West". I admit, I was a little surprised to get a passing grade at all, because the teacher wouldn't let me read my poem to the class.

I didn't know what to think about my chances hardly after Jamie told me what he did about the teacher's response. Me and him had just got off the school grounds, when Jamie remembered that he forgot to get his pea shooter back from Old Lady Showalter, after school was out for the day. He ran back to fetch his "innocent toy". He wasn't gone long, because the teachers don't put up no fuss about giving you back your property, which they have kept "safe for you" in their desks, during the school day.

When Jamie got back from retrieving his prized shooter, he was kind of out of breath, what with running and all. He said that as he had walked into the schoolroom, Old Lady Showalter was reading "Mae West" to Old Lady Cunningham. He said that they both had tears in their eyes. He thought the tears must have been from laughter, the way they couldn't keep their mouths from twitching, even after they knowed that Jamie was in the room.

I remembered how me and Jamie get such a good laugh out of each other stupidity, so I was afraid that Old Lady Showalter just couldn't wait to show her friend what a stupid paper I had wrote on "Mae West". On the other hand, it was possible that somebody besides me and the author's grandson thought the rhyme was funny.

It didn't help me to know what to expect, when, on the next day, the teacher kept me in at morning recess to discuss my choice of rhyme. She said, "Tell me honestly, Frankie, does your report explain all you see in "Mae West". I put on an expression like I had just come from Sunday School, on the way to Preaching, and said, "Yes, Miss Showalter, except I doubt that the author is really serious about going up to see Mae West. He is a old man. Maybe 'Mae West' is satire." She said, "You may be right, Frankie. Perhaps before you prepare another paper, you will let me see your choice of literature."

The teacher had just told us about using satire, so I had figgered on maybe making some points by bringing it up. I wasn't at all sure I'd scored, though. The way she had said the word "literature" made me think that she might be using some satire herself.

So I was pleased to get a "C", when I had figgered I might get a "F".

The funny thing is, Gladys Riddle got a "B+" on that little one liner. Of course, I was happy for Gladys, but I was kind of ashamed, too, that she could have seen, in those few words, what I had missed altogether. I guess I might as well confess that I might have been a little jealous if it had been anybody else but Gladys, who had done so much better than me – and with so little work.

Since she had sent me that valentine, I thought it would be safe to ask her to let me copy her report. (A report on a line that didn't even have a rhyme.) She seemed pleased that I asked.

ENGLISH

Gladys Riddle Literature Appreciation Grade 6

From "Pensive Evenings" by Frederick Glover

"Grace is like a library book – check it out."

How "grace is like a library book":

It is free.

It is retained by the user, somewhere inside himself.

It is not diminished by its use.

How grace is unlike a library book:

There is no penalty for keeping grace; books may be overdrawn.

There is enough grace for everyone at once, the number of books is limited.

"Check it out."

The author invites reader to verify his statement by analysis, as I have done in this report; and by experience, which I had done prior to reading this line. I can endorse the statement.

By the time I had finished copying the report, I knew that I was in love with Gladys Riddle.

ESSAY ON AMERICA

Franklin Benjamin Friddle English Grade 6

This is a essay on America, which we have to write here at our school desks without opening no book. We just write what we have learned already about America, and what we know from just being born here, and all.

In 1492, Columbus sailed far out into the Atlantic Ocean, farther than anybody he knowed of had ever done before. Columbus believed that the Earth was round, like a ball, instead of flat like a cowpie, the way it looks like it is.

It turned out that Columbus was right about the world being like a ball, but it was lucky for him that this big country was in his way before he could get to India. We all say that Columbus discovered America – that may be true, but America saved Columbus and all of his men from being drowned in the ocean, or starving to death. They could never have made it all the way to India, without no stopovers for fresh water and food. I also think we should honor all of them sailors, whose names we don't even know, for not cutting Columbus' throat and sailing back to Spain; when they had already been at sea longer than their captain had said they would and they hadn't even seen no land.

This is the land of the free and the home of the braves. Braves is what we call them free American natives that Columbus thought was Indians. I don't know how he guessed so right about their names, when he was so wrong about where he was at. Them people was Indians alright, but they was not Indians from India. They was American Indians. And they was free and brave; and this was their home.

It was lucky for the American Indians, too, that they was discovered by Europeans like they was. They got to learn about the white man's laws, and justice and all. If it wasn't for the white man, them braves would never have learned to read about all of the advantages that the white man had over the red man.

Before the white man came to these shores, the red man just fished and hunted, and gathered wild grapes and berries – mostly things the white man did only after he had worked long and hard at his chores and earned a good vacation.

Before the white man came to this country, the red tribes would sometimes go to war with each other. They fought with strong bows and straight, swift arrows; they fought with funny looking hatchets that they called tomahawks. They killed each other by the tens, or even by the hundreds, and scalped their fallen enemies with their tomahawks. After they was civilized by the white man, the red man learned to use guns, and to kill each other by the thousands.

At first the dealings between the red man and the white man was friendly. The Indians taught the white man to plant maize and pumpkins. The Europeans gave the Indians glass beads and trinkets, and smallpox.

After a while some of them red men noticed that the white men might be getting the best of them in the trades. The white men built towns and put up barricades to keep the Indians from hunting and fishing in some of the places where they had hunted and fished before. Not only this; but the very land on which the red man had showed the white man how to plant corn and squash and stuff, the white man said now belonged to him. No Reds allowed!

Things got kind of nasty after that, but the white man finally showed the Indians who was boss. Today, on the Indian reservations, the little red children go to school, where they learn to read and write. Now they can read about how to be civilized and follow law and order, like the white man.

Some of them little red children might get to take vacations from school, when they can fish and hunt like their great-great-great-granddaddies did. Except they have to do it on the reservation. The best hunting and fishing spots are for the white men, who can afford it. That is the American way.

CHICKEN HAWK

Me and Jamie was at his house one day, shooting marbles under a chinaberry tree. This is a real good place to shoot marbles, because the ground is bare of grass, under the tree, and can be swept clean for our games.

We do have to be careful, though, because the chickens are allowed to run free at the Klinghopper place. Chickens is apt to leave them little white and gray piles of manure around, like fancy calling cards, about everywhere they go. In other words, chickens don't go nowheres to go, they just go, where they are. They are under the chinaberry tree a lot.

After we take a shingle, or some other piece of wood, and move the chicken manure away, we will sweep the place smooth for our circle, and have a really nice place to shoot our cat's-eyes.

We never play for keeps. It wouldn't be any fun to play for the purpose of depriving my friend of his marbles. It would be downright foolish for me to play Jamie for keeps, unless I had some marbles I wanted to give up. Jamie is real good at that game of marbles. What we do is to play until Jamie has all the marbles: then we divide them equally at the end of the game.

If we discover a real good shooter, we take that for ourselves, and that marble never becomes part of the common stock. Sometimes, Jamie will get some new marbles at the store, and divide with me. Sometimes, I will buy some extra ones, and share them with Jamie. This is not so unselfish as it must have seemed to our teacher, when Jamie told about it in a essay at school. Jamie got a "D+" on his paper, with a note from the teacher which said how nice it was that we shared like that. It's just that me and Jamie are together so much that when one of us gives something to the other, it's not really giving it away at all.

We consider it a good game, if we play for a couple of hours before Jamie wins all the marbles; and we don't get hardly any chicken manure on our overalls at all.

On this day, I was down to my last two marbles for the ring, and it was my turn to shoot. I shot real hard, but not accurate, and the marble went a long way out from under the tree. I stayed on my knees for a couple of seconds, and watched my shooter go past two of them little danger spots we hadn't moved away.

Just as the marble came to rest, near a hydrangea bush, one of them mother hens clucked to her chicks that there was danger about! That hen went right to where my marble was, and gathered all of her little chicks under her wings. Just as the last chick came to cover, I saw the shadow of a chicken hawk, as it swooped down toward the yard. The hawk picked up a young pullet, and beat its wings real hard to get airborne again with its catch. Me and Jamie both screamed real loud, and clapped our hands to scare the hawk away. But we were too late. The hawk was so fast that our efforts were in vain.

The hawk flew away over the cornfield, barely clearing the tassels of the corn. It disappeared over the woods by the Leonard place.

I guess every creature anywheres close around was excited by the drama of what was happening. Me and Jamie had made so much noise ourselves that I can't tell you much about the sounds the chickens made, except for the hen calling her chicks at the first sign of danger. I expect that if that hen had spotted the hawk just a tiny bit sooner, the hawk would have flown away without a meal.

Jamie started to the house to tell his ma about the hawk, but he didn't need to do that. Mrs. Klinghopper was coming out of the house to see what had happened. She said she knew it was a hawk by the sounds the chickens made. She seemed to be very mad at that hawk for making off with the young pullet.

Pretty soon, the hen let her chicks come out to scratch around behind her and to peck around where she had scratched, the way chicks do. I wondered if they knew that the hawk would not be back soon, because it would not be hungry. The excitement seemed to last longer among us folks than among the chickens.

I went over to the hydrangea bush, and picked up my shooter that had been hidden, with the baby chicks, under the mother hen. This is my favorite shooter now. I call it my "biddy". I have been shooting better with my biddy than I ever did before. I ain't beat Jamie yet, but I've got him down to three marbles, twice already.

Mr. Klinghopper took his shotgun, and he and Mr. Leonard went hunting for that hawk's nest, but they never did find it.

Jamie told me that the hawk had been around several times so the mother hen had been calling her chicks like that before.

Me and Jamie has talked about it a lot, and we are agreed that the young pullet that was taken could have been safe, if it had paid as much attention to the mother hen as the little baby chicks did. That pullet was too big to hide under the hen's wings, but it could have taken cover under the bushes.

We both wondered if there might be a lesson here for us. The heedless pullet was a juvenile like us. Me and Jamie are big enough to get away from our mas for a while. It just might not be safe to ignore their warnings about danger.

We all considered it a awful thing that the hawk did in taking that pullet back to its nest for its family's dinner. It was perfectly alright for Jamie's folks to kill two young chickens when they had the preacher share the noon meal with them on Sunday.

After we studied some about birds of prey in school, I got to noticing how pretty them birds are soaring overhead the way they do. Hawks don't seem so evil to me now, there is something majestic about the sight of that hawk, flying low over the corn tassels, heavily laden with the family dinner. Just because they didn't invite the preacher to share the meal, don't mean they was evil.

DAVID AND JUNIOR

It was generally considered alright for anyone to fish in the mill pond. The pond was kind of like our springhouse: private property, but anyone could use it, as long as they did not abuse the privilege. Me and Jamie got to fishing there so regular for a while that we thought of it as our own special place.

The thing was, there was other people who thought of it as their own special place, too. There wasn't no problem, if the others that was making it their own special place at the same time you was, was a couple of spooners. They would usually just hang around the water wheel or go on up to watch Old Man Lumley grind the cornmeal. Their special, special place was far enough from the place where we did our fishing, that it didn't create no problem.

When the boys from the "Heights" came though, you knowed you was both after the same special, special place. Me and Jamie wanted the water to be left tranquil for our fishing. The boys from the "Heights" came to swim, and didn't want their be-hinds, nor any of their equipment, to get caught on our fishhooks.

Me and Jamie had caught about a half a line of bream and sun perch one day, and we were figuring on having a good mess in about another hour, when we heard a couple of them boys from the "Heights" coming through the woods.

Them fellers from over to the "Heights", acted like they thought they owned the world, I guess, when you think about it, they did have a pretty good corner on it because the Methodist Church had sponsored a Boy

Scout troop over there, and a feller named Bill Griffith had got up a bunch of men to help him look after the troop. They had also looked after a baseball team for the bigger boys – and I don't know what all. So all the boys that lived on the "Heights" always could find something they could do, besides fighting boys in other neighborhoods or something.

What bothered me and Jamie about them boys, was not that they always had such a good time at about everything they did, but it was that they scared the fish. And, to tell the truth, me and Jamie wasn't too sure but what them big boys over to the "Heights" didn't still prefer fighting to tying knots and learning mottoes, or showing off "Tater" Murphy's fast ball to other baseball teams. We just might have been a little bit scared of them boys.

There is a good reason why we heard them boys before they got anywhere near to where we was fishing. In them Scout meetings them rough boys would whoop it up with the littler boys, singing "Swing Low, Sweet Chariot", "I Was Seeing Nelly Home", or some other song they liked – and thought they were so good at. They was all time practicing singing them songs, everywhere they went.

So we heard them coming; and we knowed that they was from the "Heights". We also knowed that we was not about to let them come up and find us fishing in "their mill pond". We fastened our lines of fish where we thought they wouldn't be spotted by the rough boys and we hid in a pretty heavy thicket of alder bushes that growed near the water's edge.

We became pretty sure, before long, that there was only two of them boys, David Apple and Junior Barham. At first they didn't come close to

87

where we was. They just kind of messed along near the water's edge, looking at the ripples a striking bass had made in the water, and scaring turtles off the logs, where they was sunning theirselves on – stuff like that.

Pretty soon David and Junior got into a contest: seeing who could make a rock skip the most times across the pond. They was pretty good at that rock skippin', and it looked like they was having so much fun that we thought about coming out of our hiding places and joining in the fun. I was almost sure that I could beat David Apple's best throw; and them boys looked harmless enough. I said to Jamie, "Let's go skip some rocks with them. We could lick them if they start any trouble". Jamie sort of shouted a whisper, "No, wait. They say that David has a club house, and Junior and the other boys call him "Head". We better be careful! There may be some of them other club members in them woods that we just ain't seen yet. Let's just stay where we are for a while".

By the time me and Jamie had decided on no action, them two boys had worked their way, skipping rocks as they came, to a little sandy place that sloped off right nice into deep water. This is where some of the fellers like to swim. It soon became clear that this was David and Junior's special place – at least this is where they had it in mind to go swimming.

Where they was, wasn't no farther from where we was hid in the alder bushes, than second base is from home plate, over to the ballpark. We could see them good.

Me and Jamie never used the spot them "Heights" boys was using, to do no swimming. The reason why we didn't, is that Old Man Lumley had a pretty good view of this site, from up there where he was working, grinding cornmeal. There wasn't no windows on that side of the mill, and a feller that didn't know, would think he was pretty well hid where David and Junior was about to take a swim. Me and Jamie had seen them cracks in the boards and saw Old Man Lumley watching, through them cracks, while a duck was out there, looking like it might have been a cork on your fishing line that a big perch was determined to pull out of sight. Me and Jamie knowed that with all the noise they was making, Old Man Lumley was sure to spot them two – swimming, when he had tried to make it clear that he didn't want no swimming in that pond. We just waited.

Pretty soon David Apple and Junior Barham had their clothes off and in two neat piles on the little sandy spot on the shore. They was now approaching the water as naked as two blue jays in molting season. They walked like their feet was real tender.

At the oddest times, I will think of things we study in Old Lady Showalter's room, when what I'm doing, or what I'm looking at, has absolutely nothing to do with the subject we was a studying. Right now I was thinking about "dangling participles." It seemed like it wasn't helping me learn my English lesson though, because all I could remember about "dangling participles," while I was looking at David and Junior, was that they dangled. They was now walking towards the water, looking now like two plucked turkeys with sore feet.

Miss Showalter said that she would give us some graphic examples of "dangling participles." I couldn't remember them now, maybe because the examples was not so graphic as the ones I was looking at right now, which caused me to think of the English lesson in the first place.

Them two finally bobbled their way, like sandpipers, into the water, kind of shivering as they moved on out into the colder water. About the time they waded out to where the top of their legs was at the surface of the pond, I remembered "Smiling Jack."

Smiling Jack" is what me and Jamie called a big-mouth bass that has been teasing us for the last two years and still ain't been caught. Bass will usually take nothing less than a minnow, but Smiling Jack will take the biggest fishing worms we used for sun perch. He will pull our corks way under – but about the time we think we've snagged a whopper, Smiling Jack will break the surface, and spit the bait out. Like I say, nobody has ever really set a hook in that big old bass, but he ain't never far from our minds, while we're fishing there at the mill pond.

Them "Heights" boys was a laughing and a splashing and carrying on – having a heap of fun, now in deeper water, and I thought about Smiling Jack – and wondered if he'd find anything about them boys that might tempt him into pulling one of his pranks.

Once David swam over closer to where me and Jamie was hiding, and stood facing us about knee deep in water, and I became alarmed: not just that me and Jamie might be discovered, but, for a moment, it looked like Smiling Jack had made off with the bait. David turned and swam back to where Junior was, and I figgered it was a case, like they say about your stack of firewood, "Your assets shrink with the cold."

We was about to think that Old Man Lumley was too busy to notice them swimmers, when we seen him sneaking towards them across from where we was. He aimed his pistol way over their heads and fired!

In the newspapers you read about them high society debutantes having "coming out" parties. Well, David Apple and Junior Barham didn't look like no debutantes, but I bet no debutante ever came out at them parties as excited or as spectacular as them boys came out of that mill pond. They went running off through them woods, with their clothes still laying in little piles on the sand.

I like to think of things in nature to describe what other things look like – but the way David and Junior went running off through them woods, with their wet bodies gleaming white when they hit a patch of sunlight – I just ain't never seen nothing like it.

That baseball team over to the "Heights" was called the "Silver Streaks." Maybe somebody else seen them boys running through the woods. And they had to come out of the woods somewhere.

Me and Jamie watched Old Man Lumley tie the boy's clothes in knots, leave them about where they were, and go back into the mill. We went back to fishing and had a good mess before long. The excitement hadn't bothered the fish at all. When we left the pond, the little piles of clothes was still there.

We heard later that David and Junior were very lucky in getting home without having to walk naked the two long blocks through the neighborhood, from the edge of the woods to David's house. They had found some old clothes and rags in a storage shed in back of the Hepler place. David was wearing a old coat with dirt daubers nest still clinging to it. They were lucky, though, that they'd found some old trousers to wear, to cover what was so recently exposed to Smiling Jack, in the mill pond.

When Jodie Roberts told about David and Junior coming home looking like a couple of young bums, he said they looked funny. Jamie looked at me and said, "They think that was funny. Jodie just thought he saw the tail end of that story." Hank Proctor claimed he was in the woods and saw that pair dashing through the trees. Hank drank some, and may have been a little tipsy. Besides, Hank don't always tell the truth, so we really don't know what he saw. He said, that as they ran toward him, he thought they must have been fishing and was carrying their bait in front of them; but as they ran away from him, he figgered he was mistaken – they must have been on a wiener roast. David and Junior think that nobody saw them naked, except whoever did the shooting. I don't think they aught to be so sure about that, until they learn who it was that first suggested that they name the baseball team the "Silver Streaks."

Me and Jamie don't aim to tell them that we saw them. Even if we study some more in Old Lady Showalter's room about them "dangling participles."

FOOTBALL

One thing we don't have at our school is no football team. I guess one reason we don't have none is that we don't have enough boys that is big enough or crazy enough to butt heads, like they do over to the Yanceyville High School. From what I seen, we ain't likely to get no team either.

One day, Jamie asked me if I wanted to go with him and his ma and pa, over to Yanceyville, to see a football game. The game was to be played the next Friday night and Jamie's cousin, Albert, was on the Yanceyville team. I don't get too many chances to ride in the Klinghopper's Hudson Terraplane, so I was anxious to go. Of course, I had to ask my ma if it would be alright. Jamie went with me to ask my ma.

This was on the Monday before the game. We went into the kitchen, straight from school, to ask my ma. Ma was looking and cleaning greens for supper. Me and Jamie go along with one another to give support to whichever one is to ask permission for something. This way, if it looks like permission is about to be withheld, there are two of you to think of reasons that permission should be granted. It can only work with my ma, though, if the reasons we give are good ones. Ma don't let nobody push her in no direction she ain't of a mind to travel in.

Ma and Jamie howdied and Ma asked Jamie how was his folks, all the time working with the greens, like she didn't know we had a special reason for being in her kitchen, when we could have been outside playing. After Jamie had assured Ma that his folks were well, I told her what it was we wanted to do. She asked us just what was a football game. Neither Jamie or me could tell her, except that it was a school game and that Albert Klinghopper, Jamie's cousin, was number 27 for Yanceyville. Ma asked, "Is it played indoors, or is it to be played outside?" We didn't know.

Ma said that she would let me go with the Klinghoppers if I found out more about it so I could be dressed right, and if I wasn't behind in my schoolwork and chores. I knowed that I would have to have my schoolwork and chores done: Ma makes sure she don't promise me nothing that would let me get out of either one of them.

The next day, Mrs. Klinghopper came to see my ma, while Jamie and me was at school. She told Ma about the game being outdoors. She also said that Mr. Klinghopper would bring me home after the game. I wouldn't even have to walk from Jamie's house to mine, late at night. When I got home that Tuesday, Ma had it all settled that I would take a extra jacket and a scarf, in case it got chilly. Mas sure do worry a lot.

Folks what came to that game sure do get excited about not much of nothing. I had fun, though, because I was with Jamie and his folks; but I never did see enough to make me want to jump up and holler, like some girls I'll tell you about. I also enjoyed the hot cocoa that Jamie's ma had brought in a big thermos, and the sandwiches.

I'm afraid I didn't learn a whole lot about the game of football, because there was nobody near us who could explain it. I'll just tell what I saw, and what I guessed, from what I saw.

There is a whole lot more players on a football team than there is in baseball. Instead of bases, like in baseball, they have two big wickets, like in croquet, except they are a whole lot bigger. Albert says that them big wickets is called "goal posts".

At school, we have what we call goal posts for soccer. These ain't no real posts, but low rocks or something that we place for that purpose. At one end of the field we once used two markers Old Man McElwaine's cows had left in convenient locations. We had to get some rocks, though, after a heavy rain washed the safer "gold posts" away.

In that football game it looked like they could have played just as well without no ball. Most of them players just run into each other as hard as they can. Maybe they use the ball to help them to decide which ones to run into. I couldn't get it quite figgered out.

The football is funny shaped. It can be kicked a long way, if nobody gets in the way of the kicker. One of the objects of the game, though, is to get in the way of whoever is trying to do anything with that football.

Them football players wear extra padding under their uniforms so they won't get killed running into each other like they do. Albert told me, after that game, that the players wasn't really wearing any of the cheerleader's clothes under them uniforms. Cheerleaders is what they call them pretty girls I promised to tell you about. It still seems to me that the players had a lot of extra clothes: and them cheerleaders' mothers surely didn't let them come out on a chilly night, dressed the way they was.

Maybe them cheerleaders left some of their clothes on the bus. I enjoyed seeing them pretty girls, and them leaving some of their clothes on the bus made them more exciting to see; but I could have enjoyed them more, if I hadn't been concerned that they might catch cold. If the cheerleaders had to miss a game, there wouldn't be much excitement left for me.

The football field is kind of like you use for soccer, except it has a lot of white lines running across it, so the cheerleaders will know where to stand and do all of them things to show off their pretty legs.

I think I better not tell you about all of them prayer meetings them fellers had all through the game. Albert told Jamie that they wasn't really prayer meetings, but huddles. They get together to decide who is going to be "it" and carry the ball. The other side decides what they can do to stop the opponents from whatever they have determined to do. As hard as them fellers hit each other, I still think there is a whole lot of praying going on. I think a lot of them boy's mothers would have joined the huddle, if huddling was necessary to their prayers. Football looks dangerous!

It might not be the case at all, but after seeing that one game, it still looks to me like football is mostly just a bunch of "Knock-down, drag-out prayer meetings.

The most interesting things I saw was them cheerleaders. I might be willing to join one of them huddles myself, to put in a request for one of them. The Lord knows I would take better care of them than to expose them to the cold nights, dressed the way they was.

Albert must have been what they call a "right guard." He stayed right there where we could see him, guarding the bench the whole game. Nobody scored until near the end of the game, when Yanceyville made a touchdown. I would like to tell you how the score was made, but I really didn't see the one who was "it", when he ran the football through the wicket. I was watching them cheerleaders, who seemed to be especially excited about something.

The next time I see a football game, I'll try to get to be a referee so I can explain the game to you better. There was a few things I might have been a little mixed up about. When you are a referee, you get to have every play explained to you.

JUSTICE

Miss Showalter said that we will study about justice for a few weeks, and that extra credit will be given if we bring a note from our parents or the clerk of court, saying that we have attended court sessions over to Yanceyville. Pa has already took me to some sessions on several rainy days in summer, but he has agreed to take me and Jamie some for school credit. In the meantime, we can read or study anything to help us learn about how our courts work. We're to begin by writing essays on what we already know, then we will turn in a lesson or an essay on every Monday after that. This way we will be able to see for ourselves how our learning has developed over the weeks of study.

Old Lady Showalter sure does see that the pencil sharpener gets a good workout. She has us writing something all the time. (Maybe there just ain't no justice).

My first essay will be on frontier justice, since I have seen some cowboy pictures and understand about that more than I understand what goes on over to the Yanceyville courthouse.

Essay

Franklin Benjamin Friddle English Grade 6
Frontier Justice

When the West was first settled by people who crossed the prairies and mountains in covered wagons, there was no law there to protect the people, or to bother them about such things as taxes, gun permits, hunting licenses, or to make you go to school. You was supposed to listen to your wagon master so that everybody in the wagon trains was agreed on the best way to travel and to defend against possible attacks by wild animals or hostile Indians.

It was usually best to talk nice to the Indians even if you knowed that they didn't understand what you said, unless you ended a lot of your words with "um" and said "how" a lot. The Indians may have had laws about who could trespass on their hunting grounds, but since the white man had guns, he wasn't too much concerned about what the Indian laws might be. Except when the Indians was swinging a tomahawk, shooting arrows, or burning up his property, the white man considered the Indian to be a savage who was beneath the white man's contempt.

A Indian was usually treated with respect, until the white man was sure the Indian was no threat to his safety. The Indian got to saying that the white man spoke with forked tongue. But the white man just tried to be sure that the Indian didn't know how he really felt about the natives, until the white man was sure of his own power.

Justice then, was that you could kill "just as" many Indians as you needed to, to get your way, but not so many that the Indians got on the warpath. A lot of white people lost their lives because they misjudged how many braves they could kill before the chiefs took notice of it.

After the west was settled, every man was a law unto hisself. He carried a gun to enforce this law. If a man saw another man raping his sister, he could shoot him. It was not considered good sportsmanship to shoot a man in the back, so a good sport would wait until the rapist got up off the victim. Some of the smarter men would be sure to empty the rapist gun while the rapist was engaged in conversation with the resisting woman. Sportsmanship can be carried too far.

Some of the men even thought more of their sisters than they did of being a good sport. They was likely to shoot a man before he had knocked his victim down – much less up.

Today, if you see a man raping your sister, you're supposed to ask him, politely, to get off of her. If the rapist does not honor your request, the law allows you to use force to get him off. You are allowed, by law, to use only sufficient force to cause him to stop. The trouble is, by the time you get the act to stop, your sister may be already pregnant.

One reason you can't shoot a rapist today, is that, even if you see him in the act, he must be considered innocent until proven guilty in a court of law. If this is better than in the olden days, I sure hope I can learn why.

In the frontier days, a man could be hung, if he stole a horse. Today a man can steal your horse, your wife, your reputation, and all your goods, and still be considered innocent until a judge says he is guilty. If the man is rich enough to hire the best lawyer, he is likely to be declared innocent; and then he will sue you for false arrest and slander. If you are not rich enough to hire a good lawyer, he will probably win. If he is rich enough, he can usually produce at least two witnesses who will swear that they saw the one on trial when he was at home, shoveling snow off of his sidewalk, on the July day and on the very hour that you claim you saw him committing crimes against your life and property.

In the olden days, justice favored the man who was best with a gun. Today, justice favors the one who has the most money for lawyers. Then justice was swift. Sometimes a man would be hung without a trial. Today justice is slow and expensive and a trial to everybody except to lawyers, who get rich by the system, and to criminals, who are set free.

Today, muggers are free, while their potential victims lock themselves in their rooms, afraid to venture out. Maybe I'll learn why this is better than the good old days out west, when they would have been shot after the first mugging.

They used to execute murderers and rapists. Today a convicted rapist or murderer is often confined for rehabilitation for awhile and then set free to rape and to kill again. I sure hope Miss Showalter can explain why that's better.

PERSIMMONS

You may have noticed that most of the large fields of farmland hereabouts has a tree somewhere near the middle of them. Before the fields began to be criss-crossed with electric wires, the birds would often use them trees as way stations in their passages across the great fields. We read in school about how birds can fly for thousands of miles in their migrations, so I guess they don't stop because they are tired. I don't know why them birds stop at them trees. I just know that they do. I seen enough of them do it to know that a lot of them stop, and set a spell, in them trees.

Maybe if you was to ask a bird why he stopped in a tree, he would say, "Because it is there". Them trees are there alright – one tree in a great big field. Most of them trees is persimmons.

Now that a heap of folks has tractors to plow with, it ain't as easy to see the need for the trees as it would have been a short time ago. Just a few years back, in plowing time, you could have seen somebody under some of them persimmon trees, resting his mule, and mopping sweat from his own face.

A good persimmon tree, in the right place, was as essential to farming operations in those years, as electric fans and water coolers are to city workers today.

There are many kinds of trees that can give good shade. The persimmon takes less from the soil than some of them. And a persimmon tree has fruit.

Once in a while, you can catch a possum in a persimmon tree. If you want to know about possums enough to look them up in the encyclopedia, look under the "O" section. I don't know why them educated people who write encyclopedias don't know enough about them marsupials to call them what the people who eats 'em, calls 'em. They are simply called possums, hereabouts.

The only time you hear somebody say, "opossum" around our part of the country, is right after a feast and he is full o'possum. I ain't trying to educate nobody about possums, though. The reason I brung it up is so you could understand why them trees are left standing in the plowed fields.

The fruit that grows on them trees is what this paper is about. I just thought you would want to know where we got the persimmons when me and Jamie and Slim Jackson took our paper sacks and lard cans, and went gathering 'simmons'.

I reckon nobody that growed up in our county, ever growed up without knowing what persimmons taste like. It is almost as certain that, if that they tasted persimmons, they know what "puckered" means. Hereabouts, "puckered" don't necessarily mean that somebody is about to be kissed. It often means that somebody has put an unripe persimmon to his tongue. You don't voluntarily wrinkle your mouth up when you get a unripe persimmon to your lips, you just can't help it.

Teacher once read us a poem about a little girl who was very, very good – or very, very bad. Maybe she was like a persimmon, or maybe the poet had just raided a persimmon tree, when he wrote about the girl.

One frosty, but sunny morning in early November, we three pals set off to gather persimmons. You don't have to get a bunch of people together to harvest this fruit. Like so many other things, it's just more fun to do things together. It's more especially fun if there's going to be something worthwhile to divide at the end of your trek. Doing nothing would have been fun with Jamie and Slim. Getting a product to share was a bonus. A great part of that bonus was that our whole families would share in the bounty.

Like I described before, we didn't have to hunt for no persimmon trees. In addition to the solitary trees in the middle of the fields, there are always other trees that are laden with heavy, ripe fruit: if you just wait until after a good frost.

This wasn't our first year to gather persimmons, so we all three remembered to wear light sweaters we could take off and tie around our waists, after the sun warmed the air.

We was in high spirits, when we set out. Jamie and Slim had both had breakfast with us. Breakfast is always good at Ma's table. She outdid herself on this day. Pa had cut some healthy slices from the center of a ham, for the occasion. We were encouraged to eat hearty by Ma and by each other's examples. We ate ham and eggs, and grits with ham gravy. We had hot biscuits, blackberry jelly, and peach preserves. You'll think we were gluttons, if I tell about the flapjacks and fresh milk and butter. We was at the table for quite a while. Nobody could have stayed hungry, but nobody could have eaten all that Ma had available neither. We enjoyed our breakfast about as much as fellers could enjoy any meal. Ma seemed to enjoy it most of all. She was pleased to see all of that good grub disappear.

Knowing Ma, she took a lot of pleasure in our delight. But, I've told you what Ma is like before.

We had walked a good distance from the table before we felt like walking briskly. But we was feeling good and enjoying the good day and our good fortune. We felt rich to have each other as friends.

You don't gather persimmons rapidly, like you do berries or hickory nuts. When you see a persimmon on the tree, you see a smooth, clean, tidy fruit. When you pick one from where it has fallen on the ground, a 'simmon is all squashed and has bits of whatever it has fell on, clinging to it like a fond lover. If you was to pick up the trash along with the fruit, you wouldn't be very proud of what you turned over to the cooks when you got home. Each persimmon must be carefully inspected before it is added to your store of golden goodies. The heavier a persimmon is, the better it is likely to be. It will also be spread over more unwanted stems, leaves, or other debris.

We kept our sweaters on for about an hour. Most of our time was spent pulling pieces of grass, or leaves and such from the sticky surfaces of our sweet, but broken booty. We weren't getting enough heavy exercise to help us keep warm.

The reason the possums are drawn to persimmon trees is the same as what draws us: the fruit. We take turns. Possums feed at night, in the trees. We gather our fruit in the daytime. We pick most of our prizes from the ground. The fruit grows on the very end of the limbs, which are not stout enough to bear the weight of anything heavier than a coon. We was at a slight disadvantage to the possums and coons, but there was enough for us all.

We started getting impatient for more activity after we had been picking up and cleaning fruit for over an hour and had only a couple of gallons of ripe fruit. We all were ready to try something to speed things up a bit.

I don't know if it is just in the nature of all boys, or what, but when two or more boys get together, it ain't long before some kind of contest starts. We were the best of friends, but best friends like to get the best of their friends. If you don't find something that you can do better than your friend, you just can't feel as warm toward that friend. You beat your friend at some things – he beats you at other things. You admire your friend's talents – he respects yours. You don't make no formal plans for this to happen. That's just the way it is with boys who are good friends.

We decided to start picking the clean fruit from the tree. Slim had been reaching to the lower limbs all along. He would pull a limb down and hold it while either me or Jamie would strip the softest 'simmons from them. Our contest changed our approaches. We put the squashed fruit into the bags we had brought, and tried to fill our lard buckets from the trees. The first one to get his bucket full, was to get to take a persimmon pudding to Mrs. Peabody.

The pudding was certain to be made for her by my ma. The other ladies liked to make their own puddings, but Shirley's ma worked away from home. Ma always made extra things for the Peabody pair. We all like doing things for Shirley and her ma.

We knowed that some kind of reward awaited whoever got to take the pudding to Mrs. Peabody. That's always the way it had been. She takes pleasure in surprising us with something special.

Mostly we just wanted to be the fastest at what we had decided to do. The reward held second place. We hurried.

The contest didn't last long, because it was no contest. It began to look like me or Jamie might as well have tried to best Slim in Indian wrestling. Slim's bucket filled up fast. We just hadn't made the rules strict enough for it to be a real contest. What Slim did came as close to imitating a coon as anybody could have come without falling out of the tree. Without regard to whether a persimmon was ripe or not, Slim picked every one he could reach – and he could reach a lot. Slim ain't called "Slim" for nothing. (I started to say for no slight reason – but Slim is slight.) He is long and light weight. He may not be any more agile than me and Jamie, but he sure went to work on them far out 'simmons. You should have seen him!

Slim would stretch his long body out to distribute his weight in such a way that the stouter part of the limbs held his weight. He would hang his bucket as far out as it could be secure: then he would reach and pick. Pretty soon me and Jamie realized that we couldn't hope to match what Slim was doing. We just stopped to watch.

The more Slim picked, the more confident he growed. Before he got so tired he came down to rest, he had started looking as much like a snake as he did any other animal. He would anchor his feet way back from where the fruit was growing, and stretch out over, or even sometimes, under the limb that held his weight, and he would pick.

The trouble was: he picked a lot of puckered persimmons. And so had me and Jamie. We had had an interesting diversion but we made little progress toward procuring palatable persimmon pulp. (Teacher said we should use alliteration in our essays. I think I just did. It sounds silly, don't it?)

We didn't know what a bad job we had made of it until Slim had climbed down from the tree. He was tuckered. While we was all resting, we decided to sample our harvest. (Even a hearty breakfast don't hold growing boys a whole morning.)

Two thirds of the fruit we had picked from the tree was puckered. All three of us had terrible expressions on our faces by the time we realized what we had done. But we just screwed up our faces, spat out the bad fruit, and laughed.

We was feeling like our mouths had been swabbed with bitter cotton. But we was having a heap of fun. Puckered persimmons can be fun, if you pucker with a friend.

I apologize to you for saying the word, "pucker", so much. I got to change some of this before I turn it in to Old Lady Showalter. You can be sure it won't say nothing about her being old, when I turn it in. The thing is: teacher says we shouldn't use the same words all the time. I used, "fruit", and 'simmon, and "harvest" to speak of the delicately flavored stuff we was taking from them trees. I just don't know no word but puckered for the way a unripe persimmon turns our mouth wrong side out. Once you get that taste in your mouth, you can't get rid of it by eating a sweet morsel.

A unripe persimmon ain't sweet, it ain't sour, it ain't salty, it ain't just bitter: it's puckered. If you don't know what that means, you better take my word for it that it should be avoided. If you insist in sampling a green persimmon for yourself, get a friend to join you. Puckering ain't no fun at all when you are by yourself.

We spent the rest of the morning more like we had started out. We had discarded the firm, fast harvest from the tree and was being careful not to get any more like what we had made and dumped. We had made a pile of firm fruit that looked a lot like miniature pumpkins, for whatever animal that could stand to eat them. At the slower pace, we still obtained a sufficiently large supply to stop off at the Leonard place and leave some with Mrs. Leonard.

It ain't easy to take criticism. I ain't going to turn this paper in to Old Lady Showalter. She has told me some things that I do wrong. Ma says that is a teacher's job. I'll try not to hold it against my teacher that she says I should, "perhaps, leave out some of the more graphic details". When I protested that I thought I was supposed to try to draw word pictures, she said, "I mean, leave out some of the scatological humor." I don't have to tell you that I had to resort to Misters Funk and Wagnall to learn what she meant.

You will understand, then, why I didn't say nothing about why we didn't pick up none of them plump persimmons that had fell on the ground in the cow pasture. Since I told you how things stick to squashed persimmons, maybe enough has stuck in your memory so I don't have to explain. On rewriting this, I won't even mention that the plumpest and best fruit was left for other creatures, which are less particular.

On the teacher's advice, I will not even tell you the funniest part of my story. If I told how Slim dropped out of the tree and hit the ground running to the Leonard's outhouse, that would be scatological. When you head for the outhouse with the urgency Slim was feeling, you scat, a logical thing to do. (That's the way I'll try to remember what the word

109

means: When you tell about scatting to the outhouse, that's scatological. Teacher calls that, "word association").

Ma really was delighted with what we brought back to the house. She divided our stock into four equal portions. We kept a portion for the Peabodys. Slim and Jamie each was to take a portion to their mas.

We told Ma about our contest – about the bad fruit and all. She enjoyed our story and agreed to let Slim deliver the persimmon pudding to Mrs. Peabody the next day. Ma said, "If you boys will help me, we can puree all of the persimmons here. There's no need for all of us to have colanders and such to clean up."

With us all helping, it was a breeze. We soon had enough pulp expressed that Jamie went with it to Mrs. Leonard's to trade it for the whole persimmons we had just left. He got there before Mrs. Leonard had started working with them, so Ma's idea worked fine. Slim and Jamie went home soon with persimmon pulp in their cleaned-up lard cans.

I ain't giving no cooking lessons or nothing, but, in addition to fixing a paper to turn in at school, I wanted you to know the kind of ma I have – and the kind of friends.

CONTEST WINNERS

Boys ain't the only ones who indulge in contests among friends. I ain't seen a cook that didn't try to be the best cook at something or other that they make. They begin to specialize in something as soon as they are complimented on a dish a sufficient number of times to give them confidence that they can count on receiving praise for their efforts. That's why you got to be careful what you say to cooks just getting started. If you don't like what they cook, they cry. If you do like it, they fix you some more.

Compliment a cook with caution. Don't ever criticize a cook. A cook is never to blame if the bread is burned. "The oven was too hot". If the cake failed to rise, "You can't rely on that stove". You want to stay honest, but find something besides the cook that can be blamed for any failures in the kitchen. One reason Slim wanted to win our contest was Mrs. Peabody's peanut brittle. Almost everybody in the county knows that, when it comes to candies, Mrs. Peabody makes them best. Nobody makes peanut brittle that can match hers. Slim was nearly certain to get some candy when he dropped off the persimmon pudding Ma made.

Ma was famous for pound cake. She was an acknowledged master in the kitchen. The pudding she was making was almost guaranteed to be mouth-watering perfect.

Maxine, Slim's sister was becoming known for coconut layer cakes. And she wasn't afraid to put her chocolate pies up against anybody's. Slim wasn't Slim for lack of good eating: Maxine had learned to cook from her ma. I look forward to sampling something from Mrs. Jackson's table, every time I go to their house. Nobody cooks better than Ma. Mrs. Jackson cooks different. One of the advantages of being a growing boy is that you can always find room for something different.

The competition between the women was friendly, and a benefit to all of us. A little praise to the cook could get you seconds of what was sampled and a guarantee that other things would be offered at the earliest opportunity. It is interesting how the women share favorite recipes with the competition. They consider it an honor to be asked how something is made. They will generally give a list of all ingredients, cooking times and temperatures, and all. All, that is, except the very item that is most essential to the delicate difference between adequate and fantastic results. You may have observed how pleased a woman is when told that her recipe has been tried, but her product remains unequaled.

I'm talking about Christian women, who are careful not to tell an untruth. When a women in Ma's circle asks for the recipe for Ma's pound cake, she gets it. I suppose that, by now, every one of them women has at least one of Ma's recipes for pound cake. Nobody can make a cake to match my Ma's. She is as pleased as she can be that this is so, but she'll go over the procedure of how they are made, step by step after somebody has tried a recipe and failed to get the scrumptious flavor and fine texture that Ma's cakes always have.

But Ma leaves out one item in her list.

A good cook doesn't expect, or want to be told to use clean utensils and the finest flour, eggs, sugar, and butter. These women all cook for someone they love. It would be an insult to suggest that such fundamental

112

instructions were required. They are already good cooks, possibly famous for another recipe.

There may be an analogy in baseball. A three hundred hitter might ask his coach what he could do to improve his hitting. The coach would not insult the player by telling him to keep his eye on the ball. Nobody gets to be a three hundred hitter without having learned that. There are some things that should be assumed in the interchange of recipes among cooks.

I have heard ladies tell Ma that her stove must do a better job on pound cake than their stove. I've heard others say that our hens must lay just the best eggs for pound cakes. I've heard them speculate about where Ma gets her special sugar. Not a few of them women have changed brands of flour to match Ma's brand. I ain't never heard one of them women admit that my ma is just the best cook in the county!

What Ma puts into her cooking that she never mentions is heaping helpings of love. She would never suggest that her friends put less love into their work.

I was at the barbershop one day when Charlie Applewhite told about a woman over to the Semora community who had a reputation for making excellent pound cakes. The woman lost her husband in a tractor accident about a year ago. Soon after her husband was buried, she learned that she was diabetic.

The lady lost, within a short time, two reasons to continue her cake baking. She soon became even more active in supplying cakes to friends and neighbors. She needed to be needed. Her cakes were a source of pride. They became essential to her feeling good about her worth to the community.

The widder lady in Semora suffered a bout with the flu. Soon after, folks began to taste a distinct difference in the quality of her cakes. Some hinted that the old lady had lost her skill due to the tragic events in her life.

One kind neighbor detected the truth. She told the lady frankly that somebody had put salt in her sugar bowl. It turned out that the salt in the sugar bowl occurred by accident, while the widder was ill and being looked after by neighbors. When Charlie told the story it got a good laugh. It must not have been at all funny to the proud cook in Semora.

Good cooking requires the finest of ingredients. The finest of these is love. When we eat Ma's cooking, we know that we have the benefit of the finest.

If you go to church regular, or read your Bible a lot, you probably noticed that I borrowed part of a phrase from the famous passage on charity. The preacher said that charity means love. I can see that charity might be a symptom of love sometimes, but the word seems to me to be a little different. We love God. He is worthy of our love. When we love God it ain't charity. God loves us. That's charity.

When Maxine started to cooking cakes, we had faith and hope. When we said they were good, we told the truth. When we let Maxine think that they were as good as her ma's – that was charity.

Some things are carefully measured in Ma's kitchen. One thing is not measured. In all that Ma does for us there is a lot of love poured in.

When it comes to love, there ain't no salt in Ma's sugar bowl.

HAZEL'S DIARY

I don't keep no diary. I am too busy doing other things to write everything down in a little book with a lock on it. People who keep a record of everything they do are probably too tied up in writing to do much to write about. Maybe when I get old enough or feeble enough to slow down, I might find time to write something. If I ever do write a diary, I hope I can find more to write about than Hazel did.

We all know that wrote words are meant to be read. We also know that diaries are meant to be private – at least, sometimes. I mention this because I don't want you to think that I don't have no respect for nobody's privacy. I do respect privacy. I also respect the hard work Hazel did when she wrote in her little green book. What a waste it would be if nobody was to read the words that Hazel put down so faithfully every day, in the last year of her life.

When she died with no heirs, all of her possessions was sold at auction to pay the taxes on her property. It ain't none of our business how much she owed. I just want you to know how I came to have Hazel's little green book. Poochie Blanchard got the diary along with some other papers, as a result of the bid he made for a suitcase. Hazel's diary was in the suitcase.

I saw Poochie cleaning out the old papers from his purchase, before he had even left the old woman's house where the auction had been held. I asked him if I could have the keen little book. Poochie said, "Go ahead, take it. It ain't nothing – I done looked at it."

Raymond F. Rogers

Compared to my interest, Poochie had no respect for the ladies work at all. Writing deserves more respect than to just burn somebody's diary.

How do you respect a person's privacy, and read their private words? How do you respect a person's work, and throw it away? I had asked for a book, and I had got myself a problem. I decided to ask Ma about it.

Ma suggested that I should read the book cautiously. She said that I should read only so far as I thought the writer would be pleased to have me read. I should repeat only what I thought the writer would be pleased to have made public. I should judge by the contents of the book.

I was glad for Ma's suggestion. I was anxious to begin reading. I was disappointed at what I read. The old lady must have had few, if any, friends and visitors. Her whole life seemed to revolve around her physical being. It may have been different in her youth, but her life was extremely dull. I found nothing that seemed to be worth reading. Why did she write?

I told you once that I tried to be honest with you. You should know that Hazel is not the real name of the dull old lady. Even leaving her nameless may not be the best thing to do, but it's a hard question. If I name her at all, it will be for something I think she would be proud of. I don't see how she could be proud of what I read in her diary.

Hazel complained a lot. Her complaints was about minor things. She complained that she had no cushion to sit on when she did the milking.

Pa says you shouldn't judge a man until you have hoed in his row and plowed with his mule. I ain't rightly in no position to pass judgment, but it seems to me that instead of complaining about not having a cushion, Hazel should have been thankful that she had a cow.

Hazel's complaints ran in patterns. She would have one thing on her mind for a couple of days, then switch to another complaint on the third day. She wrote the same thing over so many times that she could have made it easier to write and to read if she would have referred to complaints by number: "Today is Tuesday. See #6."

Like Pa says, I shouldn't judge. I guess Hazel didn't know how repetitious things would be. Poor Hazel.

I don't know why Hazel couldn't go to church. Whatever the reason, she missed it. I know she missed going to church because every few days she would say that she wasn't regular.

"Today my stool was hard again."

"I'm not regular"

"Today I took something to soften my stool."

" I took something to soften my stool yesterday, and have been running back and forth all day."

If taking a cushion to the barn made that much difference to her enjoyment, why didn't Hazel just leave the cushion in the barn?

There was a lot of entries in the book about what Hazel had to eat, how it was prepared and such. Mostly she would say how what she ate would effect her stool. She must have been a skinny thing, to have been so concerned. It don't take long to milk one cow.

So you see how dull the diary was.

That's why I don't keep no diary. I just write what I think about in my Big Red tablets. For my schoolwork I will copy some from Big Red into my Blue Horse tablet. The Blue Horse has smooth paper and looks nicer. Miss Showalter never sees what I write in Big Red. Big Red is just between you and me. And I don't even know who you might be. Maybe someday somebody might buy my old trunk at auction and just throw away all of these Big Red tablets.

At prayer time I got to feeling guilty about being so judgmental about Hazel. I guess I was still making some kind of judgment when I got to wondering how Hazel went about saying her prayers. If she said, "I thank you Lord, that today I didn't have complaint numbers three and four. The Lord would see right through that as a complaint about what she went through on the day before. We can never hide our true feelings from the Lord. It is at prayer time that our motivations become so transparent to us. We know we are wrong, but can't see how to make it right.

We try to pray that God's will be done. We'll bear our cross, but all the time we don't want Him to lay nothing really heavy on us. Maybe it's easy to judge others because we have never borne a really heavy burden. The Lord's reasons are His own, but often it is in old age that burdens get heaviest. Maybe we ought to pray, "Lay it on me, Lord, while I am in the vigor of youth – before I become infirm with age." Maybe we should, but we can't hide from the Lord the hope that His will does not include that.

Hazel's diary is so dull, I don't think I do her any honor to repeat more of it. Besides: there is always the chance that I might tell something intimate and personal, that she would want kept private.

I like my privacy – but I do hope somebody reads what I have wrote before they decide to chunk it all into the junk heap.

By the time that happens, I'll be gone. I'll be concerned about other records – other things.

After such thoughts, how comforting it is to thank God for His grace. He'll work it out. I can sleep secure, in the comfortable embrace of His love.

CATS AND KITTENS

Our tom cat has personality. I would say that Tom has catanality, except I can't find that word nowheres in the dictionary, and I have looked under every spelling I can think of. If there ain't no word in the dictionary that means that one cat has traits of behavior that is distinctive, it must be because neither Mr. Funk nor Mr. Wagnall ever had a cat. There is a word that sounds like it could me to be like Tom, but it don't mean nothing like it seems like it should. Tom is a cat that could be a tonic to anybody who ain't catatonic; but to be catatonic means you can't be reached, by a cat or nothing. Tom can reach you.

Other people also claim that their cats are distinctive. I think that Tom is distinctively distinctive. He has personality. Tom is proud. Now, I don't mean that other cats ain't proud too. I just mean that Tom is so proud that he can look real haughty and disdainful of mere people.

The thing is that Tom don't consider it to be beneath his dignity to beg from us commoners. He'll purr and rub up against your leg, almost hugging your leg with his chin, and he'll not be the least bit embarrassed by his behavior. As soon as he gets what he wants, he'll return to his regal stance as if to say, "I knowed you would serve me. I'm irresistible!"

Another way Tom differs from most cats is that he will share the food in his dish with the birds. I have seen mockingbirds eat from one side of his dish, while Tom ate from the other. I don't know how word got out to the bird population that Tom makes no threatening gesture toward a bird. Ma said it might have been because Tom learned as a kitten that she liked the little feathered creatures.

Whatever the reason, Tom was sure a lot different from Tippy, a female cat that we fed earlier. Tippy acted like she thought that birds was put on the Earth to be part of her personal larder. She was as fond of bird meat as preachers is supposed to be of fried chicken.

It didn't bother Tippy none that she knowed I didn't want her to catch birds. After I scolded her for catching them pretty little things, she did begin to respect my wishes enough to stop bringing her trophies to the back porch. After she learned that I wasn't near so proud of her achievements as she was, I began to find little traces of her predations all about in the yard.

We fed her well, but it didn't seem to affect her habit of killing prey. Cats don't kill just to eat. Tippy acted like it was her calling to kill small animals. She killed snakes, moles, mice, squirrels, bugs, and birds. Maybe one reason they are called cats is that there is a whole catalog of things on their menu. They sure ain't no vegetarians!

You could tell when the birds knowed that Tippy was about by the sounds that they made. I have wondered whether cats thought that birds always make them sounds. I guess them birds is yelling at each other to look out when they see a cat. I think now, that Tippy might have used the bird's calls against them. I used to watch her stalking them birds. She seemed to know exactly when to advance toward her prey without being discovered. As long as she didn't hear the bird's alarms, she knowed that she hadn't been spotted yet.

I don't remember ever seeing where Tippy killed a blue jay. I've seen her climb toward their nests in a tree, but I ain't ever knowed her to succeed in reaching the young. Them jay birds act like war on cats was in their charter, when they was launched into the bird world. The jays dive towards a cat's head, and I've heard sounds like they might have made contact, but they are so fast that I could never tell if they'd pecked the cat on the head. I've seen scars on Tippy's head, but I ain't sure they was made by no bird's beak. Blue jays dive, one after the other, sometimes calling on their neighbors for help. I used to see Tippy flip quickly onto her back and strike at the birds as they made a pass at her. I never did see her bring one down.

Tom will sometimes not be seen about our place for up to three weeks at a time. I ain't never been worried about Tom not having enough to eat, but I was worried the first time that he left like that, that he might be lost. Pa said not to worry, and explained a little about cats' mating habits. It seemed to me, after Pa's talk, that Tom was gone so much that he must have tried to mate with every female cat in the county.

During one of Tom's absences, a female cat took up residence at our place. She ate all of the food in Tom's dish and hung around like she had every right to expect us to refill the dish for her. She had come to the right place. I thought at first that she was just a very fat cat, but I soon saw that she was swollen with expectation. After about four days, we didn't see her for a couple of days, and then she was back at the dish eating again. She looked more like she needed to eat this time, because she was sleek and lean.

Me and Jamie set out to try to find the kittens. Where they was, was under the barn. We could see, plain as day, that there was where the mama cat kept going when she had finished her meals; but we couldn't get to the little ones. We were hoping to see them before their eyes opened.

On about the third day, we was out on the porch, putting together a jigsaw puzzle, when we saw the mama cat come out from under the barn with a kitten in its mouth.

I guess if you ain't never seen this for yourself, you can't know the feeling we had at the sight of that cat moving her kittens. Something swelled up inside of us that we would have probably taken for pride, except that what caused the swelling was not nothing we had done. Me and Jamie must have both felt the same way, and we have tried to figger out what it was that swelled up in us that way. We decided that it must be wonder. It is as though God has given to mama cats the wisdom to care for little kittens, which is superior to man's wisdom to care for kittens.

Anyways, we were determined to find out where the wise mama was taking them kittens. We stayed where we was on the porch, until the cat had gone into the barn through the open doorway.

We borrowed a trick from the cat family, the way we moved by stages closer to the door of the barn. We went first to the hickory grove, and peeked around the trees to wait for the mama to come back for another kitten. We was hoping that we'd seen her move the first baby.

Pretty quick, we saw the cat come back to the barn opening and look around to the side where she had first showed up with the kitty. As soon as she went under the barn, me and Jamie hurried quietly to the barn and went inside. We crouched in the shadows, just inside the barn, and waited. We was hoping that the cat still hadn't heard or seen us. It didn't seem like we had made a sound.

It wasn't long before we saw the star of our show come back into the barn with another kitten dangling from its mouth. She looked directly at me and Jamie as if to say, "You can look, but don't touch", and she proceeded with her business. She jumped up into the bed of the one-horse wagon that was parked there, and went directly to where two little kittens was already lying in a cozy corner of the wagon, on a bed of straw.

Some wonderful engineering went into the making of a cat. That little kitten was suspended by the nape of its neck in the firm grip of its mama's mouth. I knowed that the cat's teeth was sharp enough to chew up a squirrel's skin, yet she landed so softly on the wagon that mama hadn't hurt her baby at all!

We watched as Felicity, (that's what Ma said we should name the cat when we told about this); we watched as Felicity laved the kittens with her tongue, as if to comfort them, and then went to fetch number four. She was trusting us not to bother her babies, and we honored her trust. They was still teeny-tiny things and their eyes was still closed. They kind of crawled over each other as if seeking warmth.

Pretty soon the last little kitten was in the new home and Felicity lay down to offer supper to her four babies. We felt like me and Jamie and Felicity was all in a great adventure together.

I don't really know why cats move their kittens from place to place like that. There may be some danger we don't know about, in leaving them where they was born. The moving of kittens may be part of a cat's life-long quest for perfect comfort.

Maybe you didn't know about cats and comfort. If you'll just take notice of it, a cat will never take the second best cushion that's available to them. If they get too cold or too hot while on a soft cushion, they will move; but always to a more comfortable spot.

Ma made a small mattress for Felicity, which she stuffed with chicken feathers and placed near the cat's dish on the back porch. The kittens eyes was open when Felicity accepted the invitation to bring her family to the new bed.

We was a little anxious about it, but Tom didn't make no trouble at all for the little ones when he came back home. I guess old Tom had offspring in a lot of different places. So far as I know, Felicity was the only mama what looked to Tom's family for support.

And I'm still filled with wonder. God don't only bless us with big things, like food and shelter and loving parents. He blesses us with little things, like kittens.

BIG RED

I have took to writing some in my Big Red writing tablet almost every night. It has helped me when I had to turn in any kind of paper to Old Lady Showalter. What I do is just write whatever is in my head, which ain't never very hard to do, and then I read it later and dress some of it up to show to the teacher. It is the dressing up that is the hard part.

For my schoolwork, I try to look up words in the dictionary so I will spell them right, and read the definitions of words when I'm not sure I know the meaning of them. In spite of this, I always have enough spelling mistakes, or I use the wrong words so much, that I would hardly ever get a passing grade if the teacher didn't give me credit for being different. She said that my papers show "originality". That word is one I looked up in the dictionary. I believe she paid me a compliment. Anyhow, since she told me this, I have tried even harder to write about things that will cause her to see that my papers are not like anybody else's in the class.

I ain't told the teacher that what she calls "originality" is really what I have found in these Big Red writing tablets; which I have wrote without thinking about how well they might be wrote, or about spelling, or nothing.

I have already filled five of them Big Reds. It ain't always easy to find what I have wrote on a subject; partly because I don't think about writing on a particular subject – I just write what I think, as I think it; and it is partly because I can't remember whether I have wrote about something or just talked it over with Jamie. If I had a record of what me and Jamie chewed over, it would be a lot better.

Last month I started on something that I think will help me find subjects I have wrote on in one of them Big Reds. What I did was to use my profit from selling my "Liberty" magazines, to buy two more of them Big Reds and a set of index cards. (I had bought myself a "Baby Ruth" candy bar before I made my trip over to the dime store).

I numbered my tablets in the order that I had filled them, and then I numbered the pages.

Since I write like I do, sometimes I will find two or three subjects mentioned in what I wrote on the same night. This made it more of a chore than I thought it was going to be. I ain't worked as hard on a school assignment as I have on indexing them tablets. I just hope it pays off in keeping me original enough to score some points with Old Lady Showalter. I won't never pass my grade if I have to depend on my spelling and punctuation to pull me through.

Next Monday, we have all got to turn in a essay on our favorite food. My first thought was to write about chocolate cake, especially since I can usually write better when I am being completely honest. The trouble is, I already know of at least three others who will write about chocolate cake. Jamie Klinghopper is going to write about homemade strawberry ice cream.

How can I be honest, and still be different? I know that just about everybody in my class will write about something that I like well enough that they will be able to make my mouth water, just thinking about them.

Maybe it will help me if I pretend that I have just eaten all of the chocolate cake I can stand (you can get enough, you know); and I'll pretend that my head is already aching from eating homemade strawberry ice cream too fast. I wouldn't want to live on nothing but cake and ice cream. I'll write about something that you could just about live on, if you couldn't get variety.

Franklin Benjamin Friddle English Essay Grade 6
My Favorite Food

I love to eat. I am so fond of eating, and my ma is so good at cooking, that I could honestly write about a number of different foods and it would be a pleasure just thinking about how they look, and taste, and smell when Ma puts them on the table. In fact, although there are some foods I wouldn't think of eating anywheres else, if my ma was to fix them same foods, I know I would enjoy them. My ma wouldn't put nothing on the table except what was good to eat.

Ma cooks a great variety of things, and all of them good, so I could say that my favorite food is whatever is in season, or it is what we are having for supper. But this is not a essay on my ma's cooking. I have to choose a favorite food.

I have chose pinto beans.

Ma will usually fix a big pot of pinto beans early in the week, and we will eat a few of them every day until they are all gone. We almost always eat other foods to go along with the beans, but we never get tired of the scrumptious flavor of them wonderful legumes. (I looked up legumes).

Sometimes, in the summer, when there ain't no school next day, and Pa will be working out in the fields, we will have a dinner of pinto beans, onions, cornbread, and sweet milk. It don't hurt the beans none to add some of Ma's homemade chow-chow. I guess this is my favorite kind of meal; and I ain't forgetting Thanksgiving and Christmas dinners, when we have turkey and ham and all sorts of pies and cakes. I just don't believe there is anybody anywheres who eats better than we do, when we have them special pinto feasts.

Teacher says we should avoid clichés, or I might use one here concerning meals "fit for a king". I suspicion that royalty would eat fancier foods than pinto beans because they might not seem fitting. The thing about pintos is that what fits at the first, don't fit a few hours later. Pintos is liable to outgrow their fitting. I'd rather eat pinto beans than them fancy foods. Besides, I wouldn't want to spend all my time on the throne.

I seen in the movies once, where people rave about how good caviar is. I don't disbelieve that them fish eggs is good – I just believe that nothing in the world could be better than them pinto beans, when they are fixed right. They say that caviar is very expensive, too, and the pinto beans is not. Besides, Ma says that dried pinto beans is a good source of protein, especially when prepared with pork, like she cooks them.

Pintos is cheap. The biggest cost of eating them delicious beans is in the side effects. The polite way to talk about the side effects is to use the word "flatulence". (A handy dictionary is a big help). The trouble with using a word like "flatulence" is that a lot of folks wouldn't know what you was talking about. It might offend some people to come flat out and say what is so much talked about and so little wrote about. So far as I know, none of the books on etiquette even mentions the subject. Maybe this is because the etiquette books would find the subject unmentionable. I just don't think it's fair, though, that a book which is supposed to help a feller to know about good manners ….. I just don't think it's fair to neglect such a pressing problem.

I mean no disrespect to nobody, but anybody what don't believe in no afterlife just ain't well enough acquainted with the pinto bean.

It's funny how, when you listen to the preacher, your mind will kind of take off on flights of fancy. (My teacher says I daydream, Ma says that I remember nonsense things better than serious things). Anyhow, I remember once that the preacher was talking about the resurrection and quoted the Apostle Paul, "We shall not all sleep, but we shall all be changed", when I imagined the pintos all saying, "Amen". Now, this ain't being sacrilegious. The Apostle was speaking of very fundamental changes – so am I. Besides, this is really what I thought.

Maybe people of royal blood should stick with foods like caviar: pintos might make them sit too lightly on the throne; but I wish that all common people could know how good them little beans taste. However, you wouldn't want your tent mate to enjoy their benefits just before you go camping together.

Ma parboils the beans before she cooks them. This is supposed to cut down on the flatulence problem. Some folks say that when you parboil beans you lose some vitamins.

The vitamins you lose must be B12; only you don't write it B12. It should be: BBBB, BBBB, BBBB; if it's going to help, that is.

Since Emily Post didn't offer any help to bean eaters, I will offer some suggestions:

Think of the beans as being little prisoners in your intestines. They will soon start pressing for an early release. It might be better to parole a few prisoners, than to run the risk of escapees being free in the neighborhood. You might be able to release a few on parole, and keep it quiet. The whole neighborhood is sure to catch wind of it if you have a full scale prison break.

As always, the best manners is in just following the golden rule. The secret is in what you don't pass. To keep complete control, don't pass your plate for seconds, when beans is being served.

I think I handled the subject of flatulence with delicacy, almost with art. This is wrote on white paper. Since it is not like snow, some would say it is off-white. I think I wrote with art. Some of my classmates would say, off-art.

Anyway, that is close enough to the final word on pinto beans.

KICKING CANS

Girls say that kicking cans is silly. Girls is silly! The only thing that boys do that's silly is to play with girls.

The thing that makes kicking cans so much fun is that it is so unpredictable. Trains run on tracks and on schedules. There just ain't no way of telling which way a can is liable to go. If you get good enough at kicking cans, it will go somewheres in the general direction that your foot is moving when you kick it. Cliff Turkle said one time, over to the barbershop, that billiards is scientific. If you hit a billiard ball at a certain angle, it can be figgered, scientific, where it's going to go. There ain't nobody, nowheres, that can tell you every time which way a kicked can will go.

We generally kick tomato cans. Them cans will change shape every time you kick them; that's why it's not scientific, and that's why it ain't silly to kick cans, no matter what Eleanor Crump says. (If Eleanor Crump could kick cans as good as she can throw a baseball, she wouldn't think it was silly either).

They don't have no tournaments for can kicking. I guess that's because you don't generally plan ahead to kick cans. You just kick a can because it is there and because you feel good – and because you want Jamie to see just how far you can make the can go. I ain't been able to impress Jamie, though, because he can kick a can as far as I can.

We don't hardly ever just throw a can away, until it is squashed into a ball or mashed so flat you can't kick it no more.

Me and Jamie has took a couple of cans to the barbershop, so we could kick them all the way back home. We take them in a paper sack so nobody will know that we brought them for that purpose. You want folks to think you just happened to come across a can in the street, so you are kicking it out of the way – all the way home.

The rules for can kicking vary with the kicker. If you make a lot of little dribble kicks, you don't have to chase it so far when it slips off of the side of your shoe. (Don't kick no cans barefoot). The thing is, the most fun comes from taking chances and kicking the can hard.

Jamie lost a can one time when he kicked it so hard it went over the Shanks' fence. You don't face down no German Shepherd just so's you can get back your old beat-up can. That time, me and Jamie just took turns kicking my can. We had it almost home when Charlie Applewhite ran over it with his truck and flattened it. I don't think Charlie did it on purpose – besides, it was about used up anyway.

If there is a bunch of boys on the street when you kick a can, they is apt to get in a kick or two theirselves. This ain't against no rules: it's kind of expected. It ain't considered fair, though, to kick a can where it can't be retrieved, or to flatten another feller's can. It is alright for a feller to flatten his own can to keep other fellers from kicking it. It just don't seem very classy, though. I'd rather let them get their kicks.

We'll kick some cans at my house or at Jamie's sometimes. This is fun when we are tired of playing mumblety peg or marbles. We even make up some temporary rules about what's inbounds or out of bounds. Mostly we just kick them hard, and as far as we can.

Raymond F. Rogers

The best place to kick cans is in the two blocks of Maple Street which is paved. This makes a lot of fuss and will generally draw a crowd of kickers. With the dogs barking and somebody running a stick against the Pickering's picket fence, we usually get Old Man Swafford's attention before we even get to his house. He'll be at the window shaking his fist, and he'll tell us to move on. We always move on. We was kicking the can home anyhow.

One time last summer, we had to kick the can past Old Man Swafford's house three times before we got him to come to the window. He must have been in the outhouse or something, because the dogs was barking and we was yelling – making a awful ruckus. We was rewarded, though; at last Old Man Swafford showed up at the window, shook his fist, and told us to move on. We are supposed to pay attention when grown-ups tell us to do something. We kicked the can on towards home.

When I grow up I may get rich, thinking up good rules for kicking cans. Right now, I can think of only one rule: have a good friend like Jamie to kick around with.

Nothing is silly if you're doing it with a friend.

LIGHTNING BUGS

If you don't already know something about lightning bugs, you may want to skip this chapter. You just won't believe it! If you didn't believe what I said about Tom sharing his dish with the birds, you surely won't believe about no bugs carrying lanterns wherever they go.

Some folks don't believe about the burning bush that was not consumed, that Moses saw in the wilderness. That is in the Bible and some people don't believe it. How can I expect folks to believe me?

I like to be believed. So if you have trouble accepting as a fact, something you are told that don't ft in with your experience, please move on to the next chapter. I am going to tell about lights that burn, but are not consumed. (Unless the lightning bug is ate by a bird or something).

When a lightning bug is not flying, it looks like a tiny cigar that is lighted at one end. Every once in a while the light will get brighter, like Old Man Turkle's cigar does when he takes a deep draw on it just before he gets into the barber's chair, over to Crump's shop.

Now, if you will believe this part, I can save you a whole lot of trouble. You can't light the other end of a lightning bug, no matter how hard you try: and, lightning bugs taste funny.

Sometimes when Jamie is at our house, or I go over to his place on summer nights, we will catch as many of them bugs as we can; and put them into peanut butter jars. If we don't have no peanut butter jars, a mayonnaise jar will work just as well. We will catch enough of them bugs to be able to read the funny papers by the light from them. Of course, you can usually understand the funnies better if you've already read them in daylight.

Catching lightning bugs gets your hands to smelling funny. That smell can remind you to wash your hands before you eat many cookies or gingerbread.

There are nights when there's just Ma and Pa and me at home just after dark. When it gets dark enough that you can just make out the outline of the poplar trees near the springhouse, this is the best time to watch them little sparkling lights moving lazily about the trees. Ma and Pa will sit cozy together on the porch swing, and I will sit on the edge of the porch with my feet on the top step; and we'll watch the light fade away from the sky, as the little floating lights seem to increase in the direction of the spring.

We don't need to talk much. I'll watch the lights through the gap between my knees for a long time while Pa has his arm around Ma there on the swing. We won't make a sound; except Ma will giggle with delight, every once in a while.

Miss Showalter read us "Daffodils" in school. As the poet's heart dances with the daffodils, I guess my heart floats lightly with the fireflies. I know what I say don't have that good sound like it does when Miss Showalter reads Wordsworth, but I sure do have a good feeling on those nights when we're being entertained by so many of God's little creatures like that.

In spite of lightning bugs being called "fireflies", there ain't no heat in them lights to start no fires. They won't burn your hand, nor sting you, nor nothing, except make your hands smell bad.

I sure wouldn't catch bees like me and Jamie catches them lightning bugs. If we did we would wind up with nothing but a bunch of dead bees in a jar, and something much worse than just a stink on our hands.

Lightning bugs don't ever seem to have nowhere in particular to go. A bee line is straight. If you was to trace the line of flight of a firefly, it would go all over your paper. They will fly up a little bit, and then drift back down, like they have changed their minds about using the extra energy to climb. Then they do about the same thing again; over and over.

Mr. Luther Burbank has crossed a lot of plants to improve some of our fruits and vegetables. I wonder if he could cross honeybees with lightning bugs. If you could do this, all of them drones in the hives could be put to work on the night shift. I just don't think it's fair for hundreds of drones to just hang around the hive, dreaming of the day when they might mate with the queen. They ought to have to work for a living just like the worker bees.

Since I learned about them drones, and that bees is social insects, I just ain't had much use for socialism.

Come to think of it, I guess we should just forget the whole idea of lighting the way for the drones. They would have to have lights on their heads, like coal miners. I think I already proved that you can't light the other end of a lightning bug.

I read in a book once that lightning bugs glow to attract a mate. It may be that they are just doing what comes naturally. I can kind of understand that. I feel kind of aglow myself, when I'm around Gladys Riddle.

The firefly don't hide its light under no bushel. Maybe, if I just do what I was put here to do, like the lightning bugs, some folks will be encouraged to lift their eyes far above the poplar trees, to the One who made the daffodils and fireflies.

Now that, Mr. Wordsworth, would really set your heart to dancing.

SLIM JACKSON

Not long after Mr. Peabody died, Shirley started to spend the days at the Jackson house. Mrs. Peabody had got a job working in the cafeteria, over to the high school in Yanceyville. So Mrs. Jackson looked after Shirley during the day. I know I ain't told it just like it is because, with Shirley, just about everybody that is around her helps out a little. Although I think Mrs. Jackson received some pay for babysitting, it would probably be more accurate to say that Shirley was looked after by the Jackson family.

Slim, or Jake, or one of the girls would come by and get Shirley in the mornings after breakfast, and walk her back home In the afternoons. That way Mrs. Peabody could have Shirley with her as much as possible. Whoever was going to pick up Shirley would be sure to get to the Peabody's early enough so that Mrs. Peabody could leave on time to catch her ride into Yanceyville with Jacob Riley. Jacob worked as a mechanic and his work hours was about the same as Mrs. Peabody's. They also picked up Gracie Lowdermilk, but I never did hear where Gracie worked.

When I say that Shirley was looked after by the Jackson family, I mean just that. Maybe you'll understand what I mean if I tell you about how it was when Shirley stayed at our house once.

One time, early one spring morning, Slim Jackson, Mrs. Peabody, and Shirley all came to our kitchen door together. Mrs. Peabody told Ma that Maxine, Slim's sister, was sick and Mrs. Jackson was afraid that Shirley might get sick too, if she stayed with them.

"I know it's short notice. If there is any reason that you can't keep Shirley, I'll understand. Slim will take her on over to the Jackson's, if it is not convenient for you to keep her. They would keep Shirley away from the sick room". Mrs. Peabody spoke fast, and was almost out of breath.

"Come on in and have some coffee with us. I'll be glad to keep Shirley", Ma said. "I'll not come in because it's almost time for Mr. Riley. I certainly appreciate your looking after my little girl." Mrs. Peabody was giving Shirley a quick hug as she said this.

Slim said, "I'd better not come in just in case I might be contagious".

Ma asked Slim to wait a minute, just as Mrs. Peabody was rushing away to catch her ride. "I want you to take some pound cake to your mother for me. Would you like a biscuit of ham to eat as you walk home?"

I was glad that Ma did that. Every time I go to the Jackson place, Mrs. Jackson urges me to take something to eat. I am always glad to take something: I know it's got to be good.

As Ma got the things for Slim, I helped Shirley take off her little jacket. By the time Slim left, Shirley was seated at our table, eating a piece of cake.

When I got home from school that afternoon, Ma was reading "Jack and the Beanstalk" to Shirley as they sat together on our porch swing. Shirley would laugh when Ma tried to read the parts where the giant was speaking. Ma couldn't get her voice very low, but it was fun to hear her try. Shirley was enjoying it.

I went on into the house and changed clothes. I guess the very best part of any day is when I get to put on my overalls. It just makes me feel freer somehow not to have to wear dress-up clothes. When I looked under the tablecloth to see what Ma had left there for me, I saw that there was enough sweet potato pie for four. I guessed that Ma was planning on me and Jamie, and her and Shirley having some pie together; and I was right.

Jamie came over to our house pretty soon, and he didn't even bring his glove and baseball, like he usually did. I had told him about Shirley being at our house, so he knew that she would be included in whatever we did together.

Ma sent me and Jamie after the pie and some sweet milk for us to enjoy together out there on the porch. I put four glasses of milk on a tray, along with the pie on little saucers, like Ma does at circle meetings. I was right proud of how it looked, when I brought it out on the porch.

I think Shirley would just as soon have heard Ma keep on reading as to stop to eat, but, like always, she was agreeable. That Shirley is a sweet little girl.

You would have to know how much we all loved Shirley to understand how satisfying it was to be together like we was on our porch, on that warm, spring afternoon. The lilacs was blooming. Robins was busy in the yard. I guess the robins was just going about their usual routine; but they looked like they might have been posing, every once in a while, to get their picture took for some fancy fashion catalogs. They looked plumb proud of their new spring outfits.

I heard Granny Friddle say one time that there were magic moments in her life that she like to live over and over in her memory. I guess this must have been one of the magic times for me, when we shared the delights that Ma had so carefully prepared for us that afternoon.

As the billowing clouds gradually changed shapes in the sky before us, we would each tell what they looked like to us. This was a game that Shirley understood and played with us.

After we finished our pie, Ma asked Jamie to read to Shirley while she and I took the empty glasses and things back to the kitchen. When we were alone, Ma said, "Frankie, I want you to look after Shirley while I fix supper. She won't be any trouble to you except when she needs to relieve herself. She doesn't have much warning, so if she says, "I want you to help me go shoo', she means that she really needs help. Bring her to me quickly when she needs me".

Most of us learn very early in life that there are certain things you don't say right out in front of everybody. I guess it's part of our conditioning, but I feel so strong about it that I ain't going to tell you everything that happened with Shirley and me and Jamie. It's just that Shirley was not the least bit embarrassed by her bodily functions; and she was so used to being loved by those who took care of her that she would ask anybody for help with what she needed to do. I was glad that Ma had given me warning, and that Mrs. Peabody had taught Shirley what to say.

I guess the reason I have told you all of this is so you will know how much we loved Shirley, how much pleasure we took in her company; and so you can understand how it was to care for our special little friend.

We will have to imagine how it must have been at the Jackson's. Shirley would readily ask help of the person nearest to her. When she asked for it, help was most urgently needed. Delay might result in an "accident". When you care for a special child like Shirley, certain niceties have to be suspended.

Just a few weeks after Shirley had stayed with us, Mrs. Peabody knocked at our kitchen door as we were about to have supper. Pa had just asked the blessing when we heard the knock. Pa answered the knock.

"Hurry, Frank! Something dreadful is about to happen, Earl Isley, and some of the men from over where he lives, have gone to the Jacksons to get Slim. They think that Slim has molested Shirley. Shirley is alright. Please go and tell them!" By the time she got all of this said, Mrs. Peabody and Shirley were inside the kitchen, and Ma had put out a couple of chairs for them.

Pa didn't wait to learn more. He told me to run to Mr. Leonard's to get him to fetch the sheriff, while he tried to stop the men. He got his shotgun and was out the door almost as quick as I was.

I ran all the way to the Leonard's place. The light was on in the front room, so the front door is the one I went to. It didn't take no persuading to get Mr. Leonard to go for the sheriff. He had enough confidence in Pa that he would have gone even if I hadn't told him the reason. I was glad I got a chance to tell him while he was going for his car, though. I thought the sheriff might get to the Jackson's sooner if he knew the urgency of the matter.

Mrs. Leonard said I should wait for her. She wanted to walk with me back to my house. When we got back to our kitchen Mrs. Peabody had calmed only slightly so Ma explained to Mrs. Leonard what had happened, with Mrs. Peabody speaking up once in a while to correct a mistaken impression, or to clarify a point.

Mrs. Isley had been trying on a dress that Mrs. Peabody had made for her, when Slim Jackson had brought Shirley home from his house. His knock was urgent, so Mrs. Peabody hurried to the door, with Mrs. Isley following.

Slim was alarmed that something was wrong with Shirley. Her pants were strangely stained. She wasn't complaining or anything, but she had been troubled with diarrhea. She was alright, so far as he knew, when they had left his house; but she had asked for help to "go shoo" as they were walking her home. That's when Slim saw that her clothes were stained. He had straightened her clothes as quickly as he could, and hurried to get Shirley to her ma.

Mrs. Peabody had made a quick check to verify Slim's observations and could find nothing to explain the stains. Mrs. Isley offered to drive Shirley and her mother to the doctor.

They went directly to Doctor Spoon's house, where he gave the little girl a thorough examination. His conclusion was that Shirley was simply maturing sooner than most girls. He found no cause for alarm, but suggested that Mrs. Peabody should watch her closely to see that she remained alright. (It still seems odd that anyone should tell Shirley's mother to watch her closely. I thought that everyone in the county knowed she would do that).

Before Mrs. Peabody could fix supper for herself and Shirley, Mrs. Isley was back to report that she had tried to tell Earl what had happened, but when she got to the part about the stained underclothes, he stormed out of the house, yelling that he and some of his buddies would "fix that nigger". Earl was so blind with rage, she couldn't get him to listen. She was afraid for them all!

I found out a long time ago that the best way to learn why women folks are excited about something, is to be so quiet that they forget you are about. When Ma mentioned the likely reason for Shirley's stained clothes, she seemed to become aware that she was saying more in front of me than she had intended. She sent me to my room before she finished about the doctor's report. She said that the conservation was not for boys' ears. I guess it was the excitement of the moment that enabled me to hear that much about Shirley. It didn't bother me none to leave, since I knowed that Shirley was supposed to be alright. Besides, I really don't want to hear females talk, when the talk is about babies and blood and bloomers.

I've been extra glad I was a boy ever since the first time I saw a girl try to throw a baseball. When I learned that what had happened to Shirley was natural for girls who were growing up, I was extremely glad to be a boy.

Mr. Isley wasn't the only one who got mad that day. When Pa came home, he was steaming. He told us that the sheriff had taken Slim into Yanceyville to lock him up. He said that, in his opinion, they had locked up the wrong man. He said that if he hadn't of convinced some of them angry men that he was prepared to actually use that shotgun, they might have beat Slim to death. Pa had stopped the men before a blow had been struck, but not before Slim had been severely intimidated and frightened. Pa said that when he saw the rage in some of the men's faces, he was scared too. He was afraid of what they might do, and he knew what he would do if anybody made another move toward Slim.

Pa was boiling. The sheriff had locked up the victim, and treated the abusers as though they were due all of the respect the sheriff's elective office could afford. Pa had told the sheriff that Slim had been assaulted, but the angry men were believed more than Pa or Slim.

Pa repeated the accusation against the men, but the sheriff put handcuffs on Slim and said, "Look around you, nigger, you don't want to charge any of these gentlemen with assault, do you?" Slim had answered, "No sir", and he went meekly with the sheriff.

Shirley stayed with Ma and me while Pa took Mrs. Peabody to the courthouse to try to get Slim released. It didn't do no good that night, but Pa was back at the courthouse early the next morning, and he brought Slim back to his family. Pa said it had been easy to get Slim released as soon as he got to talk to somebody with some sense.

You may have noticed that I ain't called the name of that sheriff. I'm trying to forget it. Pa says he wants to remember the name so he will never vote for that man for any office. I think that will hold true for most of the voters at the Baptist and Methodist churches. Some of the men who should have been arrested that night just might vote against that sheriff. Them that knowed the Jacksons was downright ashamed of what they had done. For a while after that, when you saw one of them men at the barbershop or anywheres, they looked like they might have just been caught stealing money from the collection plate, over to the church. I didn't feel one little bit sorry for them neither.

They must have tried to pretend, over to the courthouse that, since no charges had been filed, no harm had been done. That could not have been a just conclusion. Slim had spent a night in jail. Most of the folks in the county don't have no idea what fine folks the Jackson family is. It seemed like a lot of people believed that Slim had to be guilty of something to have been locked up like that.

Slim has moved away to Detroit to try to make a living. He just couldn't find enough odd jobs in our county to make it possible for him to stay.

After the injustice done to Slim (really to our whole neighborhood), I ain't sure I can listen to any court cases like the teacher said we should. We ain't supposed to hold no grudges, but I hope the Lord will forgive me if I stay mad at that sheriff for a few years, or at least until Slim comes back here to live.

BERRY PICKING

Ma and Pa invited several people to get together at our house to go berry picking this Fourth of July. I was glad when I learned that the Jackson family had been invited to come, but I was disappointed when I saw that Slim didn't come with Mrs. Jackson and Maxine.

Pa had talked to the neighbors the week before, and we had permission to pick berries anywheres we could find them for as far as we were likely to go. Anybody what wanted to pick some of their own berries just picked them ahead of us, or took a chance that there would still be plenty to ripen after our big day.

Me and Jamie scouted Mr. Leonard's farm, the Klinghopper place, and the Peabody farm as far as the paved highway. We didn't cross the highway because we knowed that Shirley was supposed to go with us and we knowed that her ma wouldn't want her to cross the main road. We tried to find the spots with the plumpest berries that was likely to be ripe on the Fourth. We started scouting on Monday before the Fourth on Wednesday.

On the holiday, we got together at the picnic table near the springhouse pretty soon after we had ate dinner. Ma had plenty of cool lemonade and some cookies and gingerbread. Pa had bought some ice at the ice house in Yanceyville and was going to crank the ice cream freezer while the rest of us was picking berries. Ma had already mixed three flavors of the fixings for the ice cream. We was to have banana, peach, and chocolate. Since I knowed that Pa had already set aside some early melons for the occasion, I expected everybody to find something that they would like on the picnic table when we came back with the berries.

Me and Jamie was made to feel real important this day because we was allowed to decide where we would go. We had laid out our planned route on paper, but we just told everybody that we would start by the road toward Mr. Leonard's place.

We was sure a mixed group. Not nobody was dressed fancy, but we was sure dressed different. One thing that made us so different was the different ways we prepared to protect ourselves from the briars. Me and Jamie, Shirley and Maxine, and Mrs. Jackson all had on overalls. Ma and Mrs. Peabody and Mrs. Klinghopper wore dresses; but some of the ladies had brought along some wore-out hose to wear on their arms. What they had done was to cut the foot part off of the long lady's hose so they could get them over their hands and on their arms. They looked like they would be too hot for me, but they all knowed what they was about.

We had already had our cookies and lemonade before I even found out about them arm protectors. I might want to try them sometime, myself.

Everybody wore shoes for the berry picking. All us younger ones enjoyed going barefoot during most of the summer time, but this was different. Even in the hot weather, it was best to be protected against the briars and all of them creepy-crawly things what might be on the ground.

For a pail to put the berries in, it is hard to beat them little cans with a handle on them that Jewel Shortening comes in. I think we had about five of them pails that had red and white stickers that said "Jewel Shortening" on them. Some of us had pails with blue and white labels that said "Karo

Syrup". We also took along two milk pails, hoping we would be able to pick enough to fill them.

I've thought about it some, and when I'm somewheres resting in the shade, it seems right strange that all of us had so much fun that day.

Here was eight people, four of them adults, leaving the cool of the poplar shade to go out into the hot July sun to get our hands and arms scratched up. We stood a good chance of coming back just loaded with chiggers. We would have sweat rolling down our foreheads and into our eyes, which we would try to clear once in a while with the shoulders of our shirts. Yet we loved every minute of it! And Shirley seemed to love it most of all.

Now, I don't want you to think that I underrate them super delicious blackberries, which we have took pains to pick right at the point of their bestness. Each one of them berries is even better than a feller would imagine them to be, who ain't never put a plump, ripe berry into his mouth and savored its flavors as he crushes it against the roof of his mouth with his tongue. Them flavors in the berries sure can give a feller's taste buds good exercise. The way the flavors jump from sweet, to just-right sour, to indescribably perfect specialness is like doing jumping jacks with the taste buds.

The real reason I got to thinking about why we was going to a lot of effort is that you don't have to pick your own berries. What I wonder about is that I know I'd rather pick a half gallon than to have them give to me. I just got to wondering why this is so.

Ma was already in high spirits when Maxine and Shirley went skipping off together toward the first thicket me and Jamie had on our plan. Besides the pleasure we was getting from our own expectations, I guess we was all enjoying the joy that was so obvious in them two who was skipping off to lead our little safari. (I had been waiting two weeks to get a chance to use that word "safari"). Joy can be even more contagious than a yawn. I reckon we should make the best of every chance we have to be exposed to it.

Our plan was not to clean out any berry patch, but to move from one place to another. We had scouted a big enough area that we could concentrate on the best spots.

We didn't think nothing special of it when Shirley went, with Maxine, straight to the very best spot in the first patch. Shirley's ma was the next one to reach that place. As always, she wanted to be close to Shirley. I still think it was because she loved Shirley's company. She trusted all of us to care for her little girl's safety.

I soon noticed that a lot of the chatter, and some of the giggling was coming from our mas, as much as from the young girls. Me and Jamie talked as much as anybody, I guess, but I don't think we giggled like the females. I ain't complaining, though. Me and Jamie would look at each other once in a while and smile when we heard the titters and laughter. We both was tickled to hear our mas having so much fun.

Our pails were filling fast. By the time Ma and Mrs. Klinghopper and Mrs. Jackson had caught up with us, Shirley wanted to move on. We had planned to kind of leapfrog our groups of pickers, but we like to let Shirley do about anything she wants to do, as long as it seems safe.

We pointed out the way to the next patch, and, again, Shirley took Maxine to the very best spot to pick berries. This set the pattern for the afternoon. We didn't leapfrog our groups; but each time the second group would catch up, the first would move on to more lush pickings. We were all amazed at Shirley's ability to find the spots where berries were plumpest and most plentiful. All of us were amazed, that is, except Mrs. Peabody. She said that she couldn't explain it, but she had known for some time that Shirley could always find a four-leaf clover or about anything else in nature, if it was to be found.

Sooner than we expected, before we had even left the Leonard farm, both our milk pails had been filled. Me and Jamie each took a pail and went back to where Pa was making the ice cream. We hadn't expected to need more containers, so I had to go to the house to fetch a couple of dish pans for our harvest. I also got another milk pail, so I could take fresh spring water to the pickers.

Pa had been churning, in turn, three different ice cream freezers. He said that he wouldn't be able to keep this up when the cream began to stiffen. Pa suggested that me and Jamie stay to turn the freezers, while he took the water and the pails back to the pickers. You won't be surprised that this is what we did. Pa's suggestions usually end up that way; but he likes to give me a chance to consider and to offer alternatives. He says it helps my judgment to mature. He seems pleased when I can think of something that might be just as good as what he suggests. I don't remember doing that many times, though.

I didn't mean to go into so much detail about our afternoon. I hope that, if it became too boring for you, you just took a little nap. If you did, I hope you enjoyed it. If you read on through every detail, expecting something exciting to happen, like Shirley remaining calm, even when she almost touched a blacksnake, I didn't deliberately disappoint you. The thing is, when you remain calm, there just ain't no excitement in meeting a black snake eye to eye like that. The excitement comes when the women shriek and run off in all directions; while somebody else makes an effort, usually unsuccessful, to kill the snake. This just didn't happen. So I'll just apologize to you for not being able to get you to feel some of the pleasure and excitement that was so intense to me that I can still feel some of it when I try to tell about it.

When you pick blackberries, your mind is so fixed on picking these berries so that you can soon get to those bigger berries yonder, that you don't hardly notice that your hands and forearms are filling up with scratches as fast as your pail is filling with berries. After a couple of hours, you may notice that you are rubbing your elbows into your waist to scratch an itch that persists there; or you may notice that your ankles are itching under your socks. If this hasn't happened to you before, you have just been introduced to chiggers.

If I don't soon finish this piece so I can get to bed, you may go to sleep before I do. Just let me say that we got a lot of berries and a lot of pleasure that day. Every one of our families had all the berries they wanted for pies and preserves, and we still had some for the baskets in the springhouse.

I have thought some more on why I'd rather pick berries like we did, than to have them give to me. I think I may know part of the answer. I'm almost sure that part of it is in the delight we took in each other's company. If the work we did would have been pleasurable only to Shirley, every one of us loved her enough to have wanted to be there to share in it. But it was more than Shirley's pleasure that we shared. We each really cared for everyone who worked with us that day, and joy bounced from one to another like voices off of canyon walls; except the joy didn't fade quickly like echoes do, but the more joy we absorbed, the more we generated.

But we already had each other's company, while we was still in the cool shade at the springhouse. Yet the pleasures seemed to grow with what, in another time and place, could be called hardships. It gets curiouser, when you realize that a lot of the giggling that the ladies did was over getting theirselves stuck sharp by one of them briars.

I don't really understand it, so I can't explain why, but I suspicion that all of them scratches, and the chiggers, and the heat contributed to our pleasure on that day. I believe that we appreciated our berries more because we had to overcome some obstacles to get them.

Our quest for berries was on Independence Day. I suspicion that we might not appreciate our country as much as the people did who bore the scars of the fight for liberty. Our generation was handed freedom, all wrapped up in a constitution that has worked well for generations. We might appreciate it more if we had to work our way through the briar patch, before we could enjoy the fruits of our own labors.

This is just what I suspicion. I wouldn't want to risk losing our liberty, just to find out.

Now, I don't fault nobody what don't like to pick berries. Being in a free country, you sure don't have to, if you don't want to. But if you like blackberry pie or blackberry jam, be glad somebody likes to pick them.

And I still believe that we enjoy them little fruits more, when we feel like we've earned them; and we have a few scratches on our knuckles to prove it.

BASEBALL

Benjamin Franklin Friddle Grade 6

Baseball has been called, "The great American pastime". I ain't sure just who called it that, but I think I heard Red Barber say that, when I was listening to him report a game on my crystal radio set.

Some of the fellers, over to the barbershop, say that the great American pastime is really something else. When the men in the shop saw that I was there, they wouldn't say what was the great American pastime, but I figgered from what I heard that it must be tennis. Football or soccer or golf don't have any terms like "love" in them. They must mean tennis.

I believe that Red Barber knows more about baseball than them fellers in the barbershop knows about tennis. I believe that baseball is the great American pastime. Anyways, that's a good way to start my essay.

Baseball is the great American pastime.

Baseball is a pastime for grown-ups, like they play over to the Yanceyville ballpark; and it is a game that boys play, like we do here on our school playground. It ain't no game for girls, even though Old Lady Showalter makes us let the girls like Eleanor play. Eleanor don't hardly know that she ain't a boy, except she uses the girls bathroom at school. If it wasn't for that, and if she was named Elmer instead of Eleanor, we wouldn't care nearly as much that she can play as well as she does. Me and Jamie both think that girls should act like ladies, and everybody knows that no lady can throw a baseball like Eleanor Crump does.

First, I will tell about the grown-ups game, over to Yanceyville. The baseball park in our county seat is the only place I've seen a game played where there was enough people there to watch the game that they sell peanuts, and snow cones, and Coca Colas.

Pa took me with him one day last summer, when he went to Burlington to sell some of his early tomatoes and green beans, door to door. Them Burlington housewives was so anxious to get the fresh vegetables, that we sold out early enough that Pa said we had time to watch a baseball game together. The ballpark, over to Yanceyville, is where we stopped to watch the game. They was fixing to play at the park in Haw River, but Pa drove on past that park. We got to our places in the park at Yanceyville in time to see the pitchers warming up.

In a grown-up's baseball game there are nine men on each team who are allowed to play at the same time. When you look at a game, it looks more like there are no more than ten men playing at one time. That is because only one man is at bat at one time. There is usually one of them men, the one who will bat next, who stands to one side and swings two or three bats over his head and around. This is supposed to be for a warm-up. I suspicion that some of that swinging might be to show off. I ain't sure about that, but it does look like the swingers might be swingers. (A feller picks up a lot of slang terms at the barbershop, if he can make it look like he ain't paying no attention to what is being said).

Besides the players who are allowed to play at a given time, there are back-up players. A back-up player sits on the bench in the team dugout. It is strange that they are called back-ups: there ain't nothing behind them benches for a feller to put his back up against. The back-up pitchers are

157

called relief pitchers. I can understand better why this is so. By the time the team manager sends one of them into the game, a fan will heave a sigh of relief that the starting pitcher will stop throwing the game away.

I have wrote a lot in Big Red about the rules of baseball, but I don't think I will recite them here. For me to explain baseball, I would need to write in some very strange languages to reach people who don't already know about baseball.

That day me and Pa watched the game, two of them hitters got home runs. I was wishing that Luther Murray could have been the pitcher. It is hardly ever that a batter can even touch one of Luther's fast balls. Nobody has ever hit one of Luther's pitches hard enough that the ball would fly over the "I'd walk a mile for a Camel" sign in the baseball park. If anybody hit one of Luther's best pitches, it would be a lucky strike.

The best times is when a team has made three outs and the players exchange places on the field. This is when you get a snow cone and some peanuts.

When Pa and me went to get something, there was so many people in front of us that the game was under way again by the time we headed back to the stands. A batter hit a foul ball right at us, and Pa one-handed it like it was no trouble at all. He got a bigger cheer from the crowd than the visitors did when they got them home runs. I was already proud of my Pa, but this catch really made me glad that everybody could see that it was my Pa that caught that foul ball, without even spilling his snow cone.

Baseball is fun to watch, but it is even more fun to play. It is even fun when you don't have enough players to have nine on a side. It ain't so much fun when Old Lady Showalter says that some of them show-off girls can play. It is not much fun when Eleanor Crump strikes you out. It is downright humiliating when she strikes out the side.

When Old Lady Showalter ain't around, we don't let Eleanor play. Baseball is a boys game.

I asked them men at the barbershop again about what is the great American pastime. I thought while I was bragging about Pa's catch would be a good time to bring it up. Charlie Applewhite said I wasn't yet big enough to appreciate the great American pastime. I guess if Charlie is right about what the pastime is, he is right about me not being ready for it. I wouldn't trade my baseball glove for no tennis racket, even if they was to build a tennis court on the school playground.

Charlie is all the time saying things to get a laugh from the men in the barbershop. I like Charlie, but I think he ought to be more loyal to the Yanceyville team than to say what he did. He said, "They couldn't get the runs, even if every player was on a pure diet of prunes".

I got so interested in baseball that I clean forgot that this is supposed to be a essay that I must turn in to the teacher. Oh well, I'll just change some things when I rewrite it.

THE BIG LITTLE WORD

I am mad at Jamie Klinghopper. I am so mad that I broke my pencil just writing his name. I didn't know I could get to feeling this way after all the things I have wrote in Big Red before about somebody what was once my friend.

Ma and Pa gave me a dictionary for my ninth birthday. Since I wrote that about being mad, I looked it up in my Funk and Wagnall dictionary. My dictionary gives synonyms for a lot of words it defines. (I didn't have to look up "synonym" this time. I remember how to spell it by remembering to ask "why does it have two "y's" in it. Since synonyms is about more than one word, this is working for me. I don't know if it would work for nobody else).

Anyways, I guess I should say I'm angry with Jamie Klinghopper. It's just that to say I am angry just doesn't sound like it says how mad I am. I am seething with anger. (This means the same as to say, "I am boiling mad"). I will list this subject under "anger" in my index cards to make it easier to look up later; so I'll just say I'm angry, even if it don't begin to say how my senses rage against the injustice of what Jamie Klinghopper did.

I didn't get mad at Warren Baxter that time he pushed my nose into the mud. Maybe it's because, although it's humiliating to have to pick mud from your nose, I knew that Warren might have been justified in doing something to me, when he heard the remark I made about his fat sister. There just ain't no way Jamie Klinghopper could have been justified in saying what he did.

160

Words is powerful things. A word spoke in the presence of your ma can win you a big hug, or it can cause you to be sent to bed without no supper. (Of course, Ma always brings me something to my room so my growth won't be stunted).

Writing what I did about words has got me to thinking about how God made the world and everything in it by His word. Jesus is the Word made flesh. The words we use are not to be compared with the word of God: but you just couldn't find nothing better to show how powerful words can be. It's a good thing for us that our words don't have all of that power behind them. Since we understand so little, we would soon make a real mess of things.

But words is still powerful things.

There is some words used on the school grounds that you just don't bring home, except maybe to look them up in the dictionary. If you don't find them in the dictionary, it is probably for a good reason, so you don't repeat them words and take a chance on not getting to eat at the table.

Some of the words used on the playground have been used so long that I just can't remember when I first heard them, or how I learned what they mean. There is one powerful little word that has a very precise meaning that I learned not to use a long time before I got my dictionary.

Like I say, my experience with that word must have happened a long time ago; but I know that my ma was very upset that I had used the word. She was really riled when she found out that I knew what it meant.

What I can remember is that I am never supposed to say that word. The word is a verb. Verbs are action words. I am especially not supposed to do what the word means. Since I can't do it, it must be bad. Since it is bad, I know that Ma and Pa would never do it!

My anger at Jamie Klinghopper was about to go down to simmering stage, but it is about to boil up again when I think of what he said.

I told you once that there wasn't anything that I could not say to Jamie. Well, since that time, there is a few things that I have found it hard to discuss, even with him. I ain't said much to Jamie about how attracted I am to girls lately. Maybe it was because I didn't want him to think that any girl would ever be as close a friend to me as he was. Maybe it was because I was embarrassed to admit, even to Jamie, the strength and the nature of the attraction I was feeling toward girls – not just to any particular girl neither.

The problem seemed to be growing, rather than being settled by me trying to sort them out by myself; so I finally brought it up to Jamie like I do with other problems.

For the first time, Jamie seemed to be uncomfortable with a problem I had brought up. He did admit to having some of the same feelings. Then he told me what his cousin Albert had told him. He told me where babies come from.

I know you'll think I'm dumb. I had seen kittens, right after they were born. I knew about chickens and eggs; but of the several theories I had heard, I thought it most likely that babies arrived at a house in the little black bag that the doctor brought to the house everytime a new baby was born.

But, this new idea was not hard to believe: that babies grew in the bodies of their mothers. I knowed that puppies came from their mothers.

What is impossible to believe, and what has made me so mad at Jamie Klinghopper, is how he said that babies get inside the mothers to start growing.

I asked Jamie how the process started. He said it started when the parents did "it" together. When I asked, "Did what?" Jamie said that little word that I ain't never heard from Jamie Klinghopper before.

So you see why I am so angry at Jamie. He has accused both his parents and mine of doing something that I just know that my parents would never do.

I may never speak to Jamie Klinghopper again!

MY FRIEND

I ain't mad at Jamie no more.

What I wrote in Big Red yesterday was wrote in the afternoon, right after I had talked with Jamie. When I left my room, and Ma saw me, she asked me right away what was wrong.

Maybe grown-ups can carry around a pack of troubles like I was having, without nobody being able to tell it; but my ma can usually tell if I'm worried about anything worse than a broke fingernail. I guess I wasn't really surprised that she could see that I was hurt real bad this time.

I wouldn't want it to get out, but I broke down and told Ma more than I ever would have if I hadn't been so all fired angry at Jamie.

I just don't believe there could ever be as much trouble as there is in the world, except that not every ma is so understanding as my ma, or so kind and loving. She sensed more of the depth of my troubles than I understood then, and probably more than I yet understand. She knew that a lot of my anger was not at Jamie at all, but at myself for risking so much in bringing such a delicate subject up in the first place. She knew I was angry at the troubles I was having that might cause me to lose a very good friend.

Ma put her arms around me. Before she finished talking to me I felt almost like she must have had Jamie in her embrace, too.

I wish I could tell you, word for word, what Ma said. Ma don't talk like I do. She uses better grammar (folks is always telling me that what I say ain't said right), and she chooses her words carefully. She always finds the most comforting things to say, when they need most to be said. I can't remember her exact words. What I remember most is the rapid change in how I felt about the whole gender problem that had begun to weigh on my conscience. I had begun to think that there must be something bad wrong with me. How could a good Christian have the kinds of feelings that I was having, and not be losing favor with God? I didn't want to get to where I didn't think there was nobody listening when I said my prayers. I was truly fearful about what was happening to me.

It turned out that I had been dead wrong about something I had thought I was very sure about.

Ma even apologized to me. She said that she and Pa should already have told me about some things that they just didn't get around to explaining to me soon enough. She said that they had made a mistake in judgment. They thought that, as long as possible, they would let my "innocence" protect me from some of the complications of life. The use of the word "innocent" was Ma's, but I wasn't so innocent that I didn't know that even folks as good as my ma and pa could make mistakes. It sounded plumb strange, though, for Ma to say to me that Pa had also been mistaken in not talking to me sooner about what to expect in life. For this to follow so quickly after me hearing what I had took to be slander against my ma and pa, it sure did keep my attention. I don't remember any time when I learned so much in a little while, as I learned that day; most of it before Pa had come in for supper.

Ma tried to get me to remember that, when I had come home with the big little word and told what it meant, she hadn't said that the act was bad, or even that the word was bad. She had simply told me not to use the word or perform the act. It was my own conclusion that these things were bad. She said that she realized, now, that my conclusion was based partly on the way she had reacted when she heard me use the word.

When Ma had said that I should not use the word, that was all the reason I needed not to use it. I should obey my parents. Now Ma gave me some other reasons why I should not use the word. I believe they would be good reasons, even if they had not come from my ma. That word is often used to cheapen and debase what should be a beautiful experience.

The coming together of man and wife in this way is too exhilaratingly wonderful to be shared with others, but should be kept private.

No one, except the couple, should know anything about the intensity of their enjoyment (or even the lack of enjoyment, because it is not always perfect). That word is considered too vulgar for such a sublime experience.

She gave me another reason which I will try to tell you after I explain that I had to look up a lot of the words Ma used. I guess I understand the facts better after I looked up the words, but Ma had already got me to feeling a lot better about my relationships with God and with my parents. All of that love goes a long way in helping in understanding. When I knew for sure that, in spite of mistakes, God still loves me, and Ma, and Pa, and Jamie, and everybody; that I was not some kind of weird person with strange feelings, and that Jamie Klinghopper was just trying to help me as a true friend – I was feeling a whole lot better and getting anxious to patch things up with Jamie.

Pa had come in by the time Ma got to the other reason not to use the little word which has been so much discussed. This reason applies also to other slang terms which are used to refer to sexual desire or to sexual activity. (These are Ma's words. She still did most of the talking, although she explained to Pa that he might have been asked to give the talk, but it had already been delayed too long).

After Pa came, I'm not sure who said what, but they was agreed on all that was said. I do remember that Pa said that sexuality was one of God's great gifts to natural man, and that sexual desire could be awesome in its power to move people. Pa also is the one who said that this desire is so much a part of nearly everybody's experience, that not to have it was considered unhealthy by a lot of people.

This great gift of God is subject to abuse. If we are to honor God, we must use the gift wisely. Since this is the way children are born into the world, the world would be a happier place if all who might become parents were responsible, caring people. We should not trifle with such an awesome gift.

Although desire starts very early in life, (now they tell me!) it will likely grow stronger in boys until they are full grown. This means I have some real battles ahead. Sexual desire can be triggered by a great number of things, including just talking about the subject. This is one reason it is rarely discussed with children: responsible parents do not wish to make it more difficult for their children. Rude words do not fit the subject.

I don't hardly know what we had for supper. I got Ma and Pa to excuse me to go over to Jamie's house to try to patch up our ripped-apart friendship.

Jamie said he was as hurt as I was and it didn't take long to see that we are still friends.

Now that it's time to write in Big Red again, I don't hardly know how I feel about the events of this day. I am right proud that Ma and Pa think that I am enough grown-up that they can admit that they might have made a mistake in helping me. At the same time, it is hard to let go the comfort of feeling that they are always right, and will always do what is best. One thing is for sure. Since it is God's gift that it is so hard to know how to handle, I'm going to be asking Him for a lot of help!

BASEBALL SIDE GAMES

Me and Jamie Klinghopper has been to some baseball games since I wrote my essay on the game. I learned some more about it.

I've heard some basketball fans say that the game of baseball is just too slow for them. Although I know there are times when it looks like the fellers in the field might just as well keep their hands in their pockets, you just never know what might happen on the very next pitch. I like baseball, not just for what you see happening at a given moment, but for what might happen next. If you take your eyes off the game for just a second, you just might miss the most exciting part of the game.

This might also be said of a little side game that goes on in the stands at them baseball games. I have lately took to noticing that girls is likely to take notice of you noticing them; but if you look directly at a pretty girl you don't know, she will pretend that she doesn't even know that you are in the world.

Them girls and young ladies can be especially eye catching in them thin, pretty summer dresses. The way this side game is played is far more subtle (you will notice that I take every chance I get to use a new word. Old Lady Showalter says that is the best way to really learn a new word). Like I was saying, this side game is far more subtle than the one on the field, where almost everybody on the field knows what the other is trying to do. They use signals that are known only to the team using them, so that they sometimes fool the players on the other team without messing up their teammates with a surprise. It is pretty plain most of the time, though, that a batter would like to hit the ball over the fence, and that the pitcher tries to keep him from doing it. That's what I mean by it's not being subtle.

When the players is changing places on the field is when the subtle game is going on in the stands. Junior Ferguson is so regular at the game, and brags so much at his success, that the fellers have started calling him, "Seymore". He says that is why he always sits on them lower tiers at them ball games.

The game goes something like this: a feller can kind of glance sideways into the upper tiers; so that he won't be too obvious about it, and catch a quick glimpse of some interesting female anatomy. Now, I don't mean that a feller will see as much as they have in them biology textbooks at school, but it will be a bit more interesting, and a lot more exciting.

If a girl knows that you are watching, she will sometimes cross her legs just as your eyes sweep across the area where she is sitting. The very hardest part of this game for the boys is this part: you pretend that you don't see what you can hardly tear your eyes away from.

I don't think the rules of the game are wrote down nowhere, but I'm pretty sure that it is not fair for you to let a girl know that you know that she knows you are watching. If you break this rule, the pretty girl is likely to glower at you, and she will sit primly with her dress pulled down over her knees for the rest of the game. This is one of the unwrote rules. It just ain't fair to oblige a girl to sit like that and to stop enjoying both games.

Like I said before, baseball is more interesting when you follow every play, but sometimes it is hard to leave the side game in time to see the pitcher's first windup in a particular half inning – you never know what you might miss in the stands, as you watch the game on the field.

I am a Baptist. Baptists don't go to confessionals, but I confess right here in my Big Red writing tablet, that not to look at them pretty girls legs is one of the hardest things I ever tried to do. My eyes will stay on the girls sometimes, even when I go over some Bible verses in my mind, which I have memorized to help keep me from being too Earthy.

My experience in the stands sure shows what the preacher meant when he said that a verse of scripture should not be taken out of context. When I mentally quoted, "Set your affections on things above.....", my thoughts didn't proceed as planned at all.

I tried to explain about this at school recess the other day and Seymore laughed. I told Seymore that the preacher said that in the Bible verse, Paul was speaking of Heaven. Seymore laughed again and said, "So am I".

Now, I believe that I appreciate that God made girls different from boys, as much as Junior (Seymore) Ferguson does. It is just that he can enjoy his desire to look at them pretty girls like that without no battles being fought in his mind about whether it is the right thing to do.

So far, I've figgered it was alright to do anything I'd be proud to tell my ma that I had done. I ain't about to tell my ma what a strong hankering I have to see more of them girls pretty legs in the baseball stands. The thing is, I know that the Lord knows even if I don't tell Ma, or even if I didn't write it down in my Big Red.

I don't mean to sound like I'm bragging none, but up to now I guess I've got a pretty good record for resisting temptation – at least when I knowed I was being tempted. With the help of my ma and pa, and of the preacher and Sunday School teacher and, yes, with the help of the Lord, I don't take the Lord's name in vain, and I didn't steal that watermelon from Mr. Leonard's patch last summer, even though it was so ripe it was about to separate from the vine. I could almost taste that melon, I was so tempted; but I still don't know if it would have tasted as good as it looked. Of course, I wouldn't even tell Ma that I was even tempted to take that melon.

The thing is, I ain't had temptations that was so hard to resist as the hankering to become better acquainted with the ways that the Lord made girls different from boys.

You see, although I've studied on it some, and I've been to church and to Sunday School, and my ma and pa have both tried to help me; nobody ever told me how strong would be my "want to" in the matter of being with girls. I'm afraid that my "want to" is becoming stronger than my "better not" and I'll be like Adam, tasting the fruit that God has forbidden me to take – at least not yet.

So, I don't want to grow overly fond of looking at the girls. And it ain't right that I should even think of blaming the Lord for making girls so irresistibly pretty. Still, I find it very hard to keep my attention fixed on the baseball game.

IDEAS

Where does ideas come from? Now, that's a big one me and Jamie has smacked back and forth over the net a few times.

I guess I better stop right here and admit that I ain't never seen a tennis court, close up. I guess there ain't many, besides Old Man Zebulon Fitzwater, here in the county who could afford to build a tennis court, or to keep one up. I did read a book in the liberry, and saw some pictures that looked interesting enough, that I read the rules. If I had the chance to play, I think the game might be fun; but I wouldn't trade my Craftsman jack-knife for no tennis racket.

With me and Jamie, we play and work together so much, that if we didn't find a way to think together, we wouldn't get no thinking done much at all. What we do is kind of play with ideas or problems that are itching at our consciences, like flea bites on a hound's behind.

It seems to me that the way we go about talking over things is a lot like a tennis game, like I read about in that liberry book.

One of us will serve up a idea. We don't really try to ace each other out, but we do try to lob it over the net. The other could be said to lob it back, if he says something to show that he knows what the server is talking about. By the time you've lobbed the thing a few times, you'll hit something that the other can't handle, or it will be out of the bounds of reason, or it will fall short of the net, because it has no force of logic behind it.

By the time me and Jamie had played with a idea a few times, we usually understand it better, even if we can't use it to solve no problems.

173

That is why I said what I did about, "Where does ideas come from?" We've hit this one back and forth, without getting much out of it but the exercise.

I guess part of our problem is that we can't really get a handle on what a idea is. I got a idea what a idea is, but I ain't sure I got it in my head just the way it actually is. Even after reading the definition of "idea" in the dictionary, I got a idea that the word is bigger than the definition. Anybody what thinks the definition says all that a idea is, just ain't got no idea how big a idea can be. Many ideas seem inspired: like your guardian angel says, "Do this". Other ideas turn out to be so stupid that you know no guardian angel had nothing to do with it.

It seemed inspired when Jamie had the idea about how to find out where the hornets was fetching building material from. If the idea about the hornets was inspired, where was Chubby's guardian angel?

Old Lady Showalter might have felt that the idea to use her bloomers to sop up the wet floor was inspired. The pants was too wet to keep wearing, but not so wet that they could not absorb more of the yellow liquid. Recess would not be over for a few minutes; maybe the floor would get dry.

Like I say, the teacher might have felt inspired to mop the floor with her drawers: but no guardian angel would inspire her to try that with a goat still in the room.

Them things I said about guardian angels and inspiration was all talked about with Jamie. One of us would say that something might be so – the other would say it was not so. Sometimes we would say, "Yes, that is so, therefore, something else would be so".

Another way that me and Jamie talking over things is like a tennis game, is that we are a match. Jamie is just more likely to hit a ace that I can't handle.

Well, like Ma says, when she's fixing a big dinner, "I'll just put this up here in the warming oven, while I put something else on to cook".

AMY'S WEDDING

The great thing about living in our county is that almost everybody knows everybody else. Of course, it ain't possible to know much about every single person in the county, but you know which patriarch the person calls "Grandpa", or which old lady is "Grandma" to what young'uns. It ain't unusual at all to hear folks talk about a new marriage union by naming several of the couple's kin – on both sides. I guess this must help in keeping relationships in people's minds. It also just about ruins a fellers chance at privacy. You try to be private about anything around here and you will be suspected of making whiskey, or some business of that sort.

When Ma and Pa first came to the place that we all call home now, they were treated like they might have been Yankees – or worse. (Charlie Applewhite said once that, according to his Papa, nothing could be worse.)

When it was discovered that Ma and Pa were church going folks, the thaw started. The Baptist warmed up to them right away, after they joined the local congregation. (They had their letters moved from the White Rock Church in Chatham). Even the Methodist and the Presbyterians started treating them like fellow southerners as soon as they learned that their roots were not so very far away. The folks in Caldwell are among the finest anywheres, but it takes a while to be accepted as worthy of being counted amongst them.

One summer Jamie's cousin, Amy Settlemeyer, got engaged to one of Old Man Walter Brown's grandsons. Even now, it seems kind of odd that

I remember the young man by recalling who his grandfather was. His name was, Alex Foster. He was the only son of Old Man Walter Brown's youngest daughter and Gerald Foster, from over towards Danville. The Foster family is well known in the northern part of the county.

I know exactly how that bit of information came to be stored underneath the part in my hair – I heard it, or overheard it, at one of the meetings of the church circle that met at our house. Sometimes I think they should have been called the Yanceyville Historical Society. They kept up with who married who. They even had opinions about who would be a good match for who. They couldn't have been too good at matchmaking, though, because they were rarely agreed.

The old biddies were happy with the Amy – Alex match. To the circle it was a Brown – Settlemeyer match. To me and Jamie it was another chance to see a pretty girl in a wedding dress and to eat cake and such at the reception. We didn't even think about the little second cousins that Jamie might soon have.

Widder Peabody made the wedding gown for Amy. Me and Jamie was Indian wrestling back of the Peabody tobacco barn one day when Amy came for a fitting.

When the car drove into the grove in front of the Peabody place, we kept on trying to push or pull each other off balance. (I guess, when I think about it, we didn't want to miss a possible chance of impressing a girl our own age. Girls act like they ain't paying no attention to boys like us, but we know better – I learned that much just hearing the Yanceyville chatter-boxes at Ma's circle). Like I said, we just kept on tussling until we saw that the girl was older than us. She was out of the car before we saw that it was Amy.

Amy is a pretty young girl. Her being Jamie's cousin didn't keep us from admiring how well she was demonstrating the wisdom of the Lord in making Adam's companion female. Me and Jamie was both beginning to take more special notice of things like that. We was getting to be more and more grateful for the Lord's bounty. The way Amy looked when she showed a flash of thigh in getting out of the car served to increase our gratitude.

We knowed, already, about the wedding plans. That knowledge helped to build our growing interest.

The preacher will resort to some pretty big words sometimes, when he wants to be especially plain about things he has to be careful not to get too plain about. He said that we should not have a prurient interest in members of the opposite sex. I had to look up that word, "prurient". I won't try to tell you what it means, but I remember it by, "pure it ain't". We wanted to see more of Amy, and gave little thought to the fact that we were getting dangerously close to a transgression.

We turned from our forgotten game to holler "Hi" to Amy. I don't even remember who was driving the car Amy rode up in. I guess we spoke to whoever it was. We practiced speaking to everybody. Our eyes were on Amy. If the driver of that car was to need somebody to testify, over to the Yanceyville courthouse, who it was we seen that day, bringing Amy to Mrs. Peabody's to get fitted for her wedding dress, neither one of us could help a bit. We seen Amy. There just wasn't room enough in our eyeballs to have seen nothing else.

We watched until Amy had been ushered into the house. Me and Jamie just looked at each other and grinned. By the way we was feeling, we could have been standing on a cloud. Our thoughts were much too Earthy for the clouds, though. I suspicion that Jamie's thoughts were as fanciful as mine. Here we was, just a few yards from where the beautiful bride-to-be was having a new dress fitted snugly against her feminine form.

I am a helpful feller by nature. Mrs. Peabody's nimble fingers was nipping and tucking about the contours of Amy's body. The backs of her fingers was bound to press against the softness of feminine allurements. I had never before been so anxious to help Mrs. Peabody with her chores.

Our thoughts about the fitting were not fitting. Jamie didn't tell me that he was thinking along the same contoured lines as me, but I know Jamie pretty well. I know how I was feeling and what I was thinking.

We went back to Indian wrestling so we could stay occupied until Amy came back out of the house. Jamie throwed me off balance several times in a row. My heart wasn't in no tussle with Jamie. My desire was in the house with Amy.

Ma called me to supper before Amy came away from her fitting.

My hardest tussle came at prayer time that night. I honestly wanted to please the Lord in what I thought, as well as in what I did. I had been unable to get the lovely Amy off my mind since that flash of inspiration when she arrived at the Peabody's. To tell the truth, I liked having Amy on my mind – and I knowed that she was promised to Alex. I had never felt such strong desire for the unobtainable and the forbidden before. My prayers were interrupted by daydreams. I wanted what I could not have. I couldn't deceive the Lord by saying, "Thy will be done".

I learned something that day about Adam that had troubled me for years. How could our first parent have been so easily duped into risking his close union with God?

On this night I knowed something about how tempting forbidden fruit could be. I went to sleep before I ever got things straight with the Lord. I hope He ain't too offended by my lack of endurance.

I had a very vivid dream that night. It was not about Amy or nobody that I knowed. The woman in my dream was desirable and available. After the long talk I had with my folks that time, Pa gave me a book, "What Every Young Man Ought To Know". I learned something of what the author had wrote about that night.

I awoke feeling guilty and ashamed – but relieved. It seems to me that every young man needs to know a lot more than what was in that book.

The wedding was a great success. Me and Jamie got all the cake and punch we wanted. Although our appetites had recently been enlarged, we was able to be somewhat satisfied by the usual mundane pleasures.

I was able to look at Amy and to share in the communal pride that one of our own should present such an excellent target for the cameras. The Yanceyville paper said, as they usually do, that the bride was truly lovely. This time they couldn't have been honest and have said less.

As soon as the couple left the church, me and Jamie hightailed it home to change into more comfortable clothes. Then we went fishing. That book that Pa had gave me said something about, "sublimation". The fish kept us right busy, or the exercise would not have worked to keep our minds from Alex's good fortune.

I had supper with the Klinghoppers. They was enjoyable to be with. We went into the parlor after the fish supper and looked at some pictures of Yellowstone National Park. We seen them pictures through a device called a stereoscope. They was really two different pictures we seen at the same time, but it looked like one picture in the stereoscope. Them pictures made you feel like you should say, "Excuse me", to the photographer – you seemed like you was standing in his way. The Klinghoppers had just got the stereoscope (I like to say that word) – they had just got the stereoscope so I hadn't ever seen the like before. Me and Jamie looked through the stereoscope a lot after that night.

Prayer time wasn't quite so difficult the night of the wedding as I was afraid it might have been. I knowed I was feeling two ways at once. I truly wanted Alex Foster to have a happy life with Amy. I couldn't help feeling more than a little envious of the groom, though. At the moment of my prayers, he might have opened the delightful wedding gift, which had been presented to him still snug in the wrapping which had been carefully prepared by the skilled hands of Widder Peabody.

Maybe I was beginning to see life in a new dimension.

I understand more now about how Adam could have had so much and still wanted more. No wonder the preacher is so anxious that we know about the doctrines of grace. I suspicion that we all do wrong sometimes – but I shouldn't be trying to make excuses, for me or for Adam.

Amy was in good hands – but she was not in my hands. I believed that the Lord had someone for me. Sometimes it gets very difficult to wait on the Lord.

SCOUT CAMP

One October day me and Jamie went over to Yanceyville for church services. Me and him don't usually go to nobody else's church much on Sundays. We are usually at our own church on any day services is being held. On this particular October Sunday they was starting a Boy Scout troop in Albert Klinghopper's church. It wasn't to be really part of the church since the Boy Scout Council would be "giving guidance" to the troop. The church was to be the sponsor. I think that meant that the Boy Scouts made the rules and the Methodist paid the bill. I ain't sure about that, but, anyhow, me and Jamie went.

As I remember, Pa the preacher, and some of them deacons had thoughts of bringing the scouts to our town. Pa knowed that me and Jamie would not leave out much when we got back home to tell about what went on at the dedication. Maybe you remember that Albert is Jamie's cousin. Methodist must be alright if Jamie's cousin was one. I was careful, though, so as not to take any chances on converting to Methodism. I kept my eyes open, even during prayers, to make sure nobody laid no hands on me.

Them Boy Scouts was made to seem plumb interesting. They had a visiting speaker who had been a Scout in his youth. Him and two other boys had been to Africa and had wrote a book about it. I think them fellers had a lot of fun in Africa. The best I can understand it though, the Baptist might as well keep on sending missionaries to the dark continent. Not all of them natives had learned to be brave, clean and reverent yet. Three Boy Scouts can only do so much in one summer.

183

A whole bunch of them Methodist men agreed to help teach the young boys to tie knots, build camp fires, cook potatoes in hot coals, name some stars, find the north side of trees, and a whole lot of other things I remember but won't recite now. I don't want you to drop off to sleep like Old Man Wyrick did right in the middle of the talk. (I don't think nobody hardly would have noticed that Old Man Wyrick was asleep, if his snoring hadn't of been interrupted with a loud snort, that made Widder Southern drop her songbook.)

Me and Jamie got all excited about scouting. We couldn't hardly wait to get home and to begin selling our folks on the idea. I just knowed that my pa would make a great scoutmaster. Mr. Leonard knowed a lot about the woodlands and the little critters and all. Mr. Klinghopper had served a hitch in the navy: he could have the rope business all tied up. The more me and Jamie talked about it the more excited we got.

You just ain't going to understand what I've got to tell you next. We didn't get no Boy Scout troop at the Baptist Church. When we told Pa and Ma how much we thought we ought to have a troop, they didn't get as worked up with shivering excitement as me and Jamie. Pa said that he would talk some more with the men of our church, and that they would all learn more about it. Me and Jamie was crushed. If you know Baptist, you know that they can keep things under advisement for a long time. We never did get the scout troop. I don't think that the church ever decided not to sponsor a troop. They just never did decide – one way or the other.

Me and Jamie didn't lose out altogether, though. Albert was really interested in the Boy Scouts. One summer, when Albert came to Jamie's to spend a week of his vacation time, he brought his Boy Scout

Handbook. He taught us a lot. We learned the scout oath, the scout laws, what merit badges was required for advancement – we learned a lot. Pa showed Albert some things so he could earn a merit badge in carpentry. Me and Jamie was learning everything right along with Albert as long as he was at Jamie's.

When Albert Klinghopper and Theodore Baxter became the first in their troop to make the rank of Eagle, me and Jamie's folks all went to the ceremonies where everybody gets to congratulate the winners of awards. I believe every one of them boys in the troop had done at least one thing that he received some kind of award for. All of us was impressed: mainly by the Eagle awards.

When Pa congratulated Albert and Theo for their achievements, I sure wished that I could have done something to make him as proud of me. Ma put her hand on my shoulder and squeezed, She is sure a smart and loving woman.

Ma came to my room the night of the awards ceremonies. She said that she knew that she couldn't make me understand fully why we had been denied the scouting experiences. She was right about me not understanding, but I'll do what I can to report what she talked about.

She had me read Psalm One Hundred Twenty-One.

She told me that both her and Pa thought that the Boy Scouts was a fine organization.

She told me that I should look to her and Pa and to the church to teach me about God's laws and about morals and such.

She said that the Baptist thought that they shouldn't rely on any organization outside of the church to do the job that was supposed to belong to parents and to churches.

She asked, "Do you understand? My help cometh from the Lord?"

I answered, "Sort of." She said, "It's hard for us too, Frankie. We love you, and we want you to be happy."

At prayer time I quoted Psalm One Twenty One back to the Lord, and asked for better understanding. I was feeling some better by the time sleep came.

But I still would like to be an Eagle Scout.

Me and Jamie got to go to Camp Black Rock to visit Albert one day the first summer he went there. We was invited to eat with Albert and to sample his cooking. It just so happened that the camp counselor came around to judge Albert's cooking at the same meal.

The baked potatoes and the seared steak was both very good. The bread that was cooked in the coals had a really great flavor. We all watched the face of the counselor as he sampled each of Albert's offerings. The pleased look on his face warmed our hopes for a splendid dessert.

The counselor was going from site to site so he didn't eat much of anything. He lingered longer over Albert's rice pudding than anything else. We was still busy with the meat and potatoes when the counselor left. If you have had the experience of eating out of doors like we was doing, maybe you can guess how great we was feeling – for ourselves, and for Albert, who had planned his rice pudding as a special treat.

Nobody had told Albert that the recipe he used meant for the rice to be precooked. We managed quite well without no dessert. Albert's grade was O.K. for the meal. The counselor even asked Albert for his rice pudding recipe.

Ma's bacon and eggs seemed better than usual the next day.

I'm going to try making a rice pudding sometime. I won't forget to use cooked rice. If your own memory needs help on that point, just try eating it Albert's way sometime – it's unforgettable.

I sure wish I could be a Eagle Scout.

GRAMMAR

How do you spell "trocious"?

My old Funk and Wagnall's dictionary is getting to be all battered and worn now. It takes longer to turn the pages than it used to. I still can find words pretty quick, though, if I know how to spell them. Some words are spelled much different from the way they sound, until you learn that the letter "P" hides in many guises. A new word is not a "pneu" word, although pneumonia only sometimes starts off with a cough – it always starts with a "p". By itself, that ain't much to know, but added to all the other things I have looked up, I have built up a "good vocabulary". You will notice that them words about my knowing a lot of words is in quotes. I quoted Miss Showalter, who ought to know – she's my teacher. She said I had the best vocabulary of anybody in the class.

I ain't found "trocious" yet.

Sometimes you can find a word that you can't spell by looking up a synonym. I can find synonyms better in my dictionary than in the ones at school. I even learned the word "synonym" from Mr. Funk and Mr. Wagnall, whichever one wrote that part of the book.

The real trouble with the word I want to find now is that I ain't sure exactly what it means. I have just tried to judge its meaning from the context in which it was used, like Miss Showalter says. It must be some kind of compliment, cause the teacher was complimenting me when she used it.

This old book just might be the best birthday present Ma and Pa ever gave me. I like my fielder's glove and the catcher's mitt, especially when

I've got Jamie to play with. The dictionary I can use alone. I like it. I take pride in using it alone. That's why I ain't gone to Ma and asked her how to spell "trocious". I might have asked her if I hadn't just been complimented on having a good vocabulary. Compliments mean more to you if you can believe that they are true.

Ma likes to let me feel like I got some privacy. She sometimes don't let on that she knows as much about me as she knows. I like that. I also like it that she will put her arms around me and understand me so well when something is bothering me.

The preacher will occasionally talk over a boys head. He'll use words that are intended for adult ears. Ma knows that I rush home to learn exactly what the preacher was talking about. Nothing seems to get your interest like somebody trying to keep you from finding out about something.

If I was to ask Ma what "trocious" means, she would want to know what brought the word to mind. She might not ask me right out, but she would use her surmising skills to find out. I don't mind Ma knowing about the teacher's compliment – in fact, I aim to tell her – as soon as I know exactly what it means.

I'll examine the context, once again: we was talking about how I knowed more words than even Rosemary Raincamp. Rosemary always uses the best grammar. Rosemary talks like a book, or a teacher, or a parent. That's O.K. for girls, but boys sure don't want to sound like no girls. Me and Jamie are real careful not to sound like Rosemary Raincamp. I suppose that might be the reason I have worked so hard to learn a lot of words – so I won't sound like no girl, even when I get my point across as good as her.

I remember now. Miss Showalter had finished grading our essays on "Fall Colors". She said my descriptions were almost poetic. Then she said them words about my vocabulary. Then she mentioned Rosemary's grammar. Then she said again that I knowed more words, but my grammar was a "trocious".

For my grammar to be a trocious, "trocious" must mean that I don't sound like no girl. I like that. When me or Jamie talk, you can tell right away that it ain't Rosemary Raincamp doing the talking. When Old L...— when Miss Showalter reads from the best homework papers, you can always tell if it is mine or Rosemary's that she's reading. We just don't sound alike at all. I like that.

"Trocious" must mean something about how girls and boys is different. Now what is a word that means that? I'll try "gender". No. It ain't "gender", but it was interesting to read again. I'll try "better". The way she said it, Miss Showalter might have meant that my vocabulary was good but my grammar was better, because it didn't sound like nobody else's, especially no girls.

Naw. It ain't "better" neither. That wasn't no good idea anyhow because Miss Showalter ain't about to tell me that my English is better than her own.

I sure hope I don't have to ask Ma how to look up this word, but I am about to be stumped. It's almost as bad as when I first looked up "pneumonia". Say! There's a thought:; maybe the word don't start with no "t". If I can remember just how Miss Showalter said "a trocious" – I'll bet that's it! Them letters might be all run together into one word; Let me try it. A-t-r-o-c-i-o-u-s.

Please excuse me if I don't go on. I ain't feeling so good, all of a sudden.

I'll wait until tomorrow to tell Ma that Old Lady Showalter said that my grammar was atrocious.

I still don't want to sound like no girl.

HORSESHOES AND PHILOSOPHY

Last summer, one thing me and Jamie played a lot together was horseshoes. We didn't use no regulation shoes like they use in them pitching tournaments. The shoes we used wasn't made to fit no regulations: they was made to fit horses. We didn't usually have no two shoes alike. They would sometimes be pretty thick and heavy, and, at other times, real light and thin. We usually paired them; thin with thin; heavy with heavy; so a feller could kind of get used to the weight of the pair he was pitching. There were times when we would mix the pairing, just to keep the interest up.

We used old, wore out horseshoes. A proud horse wouldn't have wanted to wear them in no Easter parade. Some of them shoes was so thin that the horses owners must have let the horse's pride wear down with the shoes. Them thin shoes was the easiest to pitch and they would slide real good. We usually preferred the thin ones.

If one of us got to throwing too many ringers, we would move the stobs farther apart. (Stobs is what we called them little metal posts we was trying to hook with the pitched shoes). If we had ever got to throwing ringers all the time, we would have found some other game to play. A feller likes a challenge. A feller likes to win, but I believe the fun would go out of life, if a feller always won at everything, without no hard trying. This is just what I believe, but I ain't nowheres near being sure. I ain't never been so good at anything that I could win all the time. I always have to try real hard, just to keep up with Jamie.

Except when boys from the "Heights" came over to play with us, we made up our own rules. I can't remember all of the ways we played, but we always kept it challenging.

When the "Heights" boys played, they was all the time telling us how you was "supposed" to play. You was "supposed to count a shoe as closest to the stob, only if it was within a certain distance; a leaner was 'supposed' to count three points; a ringer was 'supposed' to count five points; you was 'supposed' to end a game with an odd number of points (like 11 or 21). You was 'supposed' to let the winner pick his pair of shoes, and to pitch first." By the time them other boys got through with all their supposing, me and Jamie could have already pitched a couple of games.

We almost always shared with the other boys. We was willing to let them decide about the way we was "supposed " to play. One thing we didn't share, though, was the decision about how far apart the stobs was supposed to be. Fellers just shouldn't always yield to somebody else's "supposing".

Letting other boys play gave me and Jamie a chance to be partners. We could usually win, when we was partners, but the other fellers laid it to our being able to set the stobs where we wanted them. We didn't let that bother us none. We enjoyed giving a "shellacking" to whoever challenged us to a game.

It wasn't last year, but I remember beating Pa once in a game, when nobody else was around to watch us pitch. Pa stayed busy with work most of the time. It was a special privilege to pitch them horseshoes with my pa.

I knowed I had a lot more time to practice than my pa. Pa didn't do nothing hardly just to have fun. I don't think it even occurred to me to let Pa win. If it had occurred to me, I don't think I could have done it. It was a lot easier to throw them heaviest shoes, than it would have been to throw a game.

We played a game of eleven. Hookers counted five; leaners, three; closest shoe, one. Pa throwed double ringers the first time up! It still amazes me that he was able to do that. I suspicion that Pa was a little surprised too. Now, here was a challenge!

After that first pitch, Pa kept hitting the stob with the shoes, and they would go flying off a long way from the stob. This kept up until I won the game without ever getting close to a ringer. Pa didn't have time for another game.

Losing that game probably didn't hurt Pa none. He probably went right back to whatever job he was working on, and forgot about it. I ain't forgot it. I don't know why, but when I think of that game, I always wind up wishing that one of Pa's pitches would have grabbed ahold of the stob.

A whole lot of the times when I think I know the right and wrong of things, I got the idea of what is right from my pa. He wouldn't have just throwed the game in favor of his son. What he could have done was to have challenged hisself to win with another hooker, or not to win at all. After he made up his mind to do this, he just might have put a little too much vinegar behind every pitch, so that no pitch could wind up near the stob, except one that clung to the stob the way a dizzy girl in love clings to the one she is going around with.

In any case, I know my pa wants me to be a winner.

Me and Jamie has played a lot of a made up game we call "philosophy". It's mostly played with just me and him, so nobody has had a chance to tell us how it is supposed to be played. We got the idea for our game from what we heard in the barbershop, and what we've read about it.

Old man Turkle ain't got much education: he seems right proud of it. He reads some books. He reads a little, and talks a lot, about what he calls "philosophy".

Now, I don't know enough about philosophy to explain real good about it, like I explained about football. Football is probably very simple, compared to philosophy. Even when I explained football, I might have made one or two mistakes. I hope you know, I did the best I could. When I explain philosophy, if I should say something that don't quite fit the facts, please remember that I don't claim to understand it real good like I do about how to write right, and how to speak right. I think philosophy is about what is right.

Old Man Turkle says that philosophy is about how you play the game of life. Now, I believe that life is a serious matter and not just a game; but the definition of the word in my Funk and Wagnall is so big that it looks like there's room enough for Old Man Turkle to be right.

Anyways, me and Jamie used some of what Mr. Turkle said to play our game. The first rule is: there ain't no rules. That don't sound right. Let me try again. The first rule is: there is no authority to which we can resort to prove a idea. That sounds more accurate, but too much like the way Rosemary Raincamp talks. I'll start over. When we play philosophy, we pretend that nothing that we've been told, and nothing that we've read, can be cited to prove that something we believe is really so.

We have played this game with each other quite a bit. There just ain't much we can prove, without quoting some authority. It took us a while to get the hang of it.

I still ain't sure that me and Jamie can play the game without no bias. We are both Baptists. When you start to talking about what is right, we Baptist got a real good rule book we can go to for the answers. It ain't really possible for me and Jamie to leave our faith in them little cigar boxes, where we keep our other treasures. We are believers, even when we play the game and try to prove the right and wrong of things without depending on what we've read in any book or what we have been told. It ain't easy. Mostly we are able to call foul every time one of us tries to prove what is right without repeating what the teacher or the preacher has said, or what we've read somewheres.

Like we use old wore out horseshoes, when we pitch them without no rules; we pitch some old wore out ideas around, when we play "philosophy".

Anyways, it's kind of fun, and I ain't sure it ain't useful. One thing it does is to make you appreciate the authorities we are forced to resort to, to make any progress in understanding.

To understand our game, try this: is the Earth round or flat? Explain why you think that the Earth is round without depending on what you have read or what you have been told. This is one of the first things we tried. We didn't neither one try to prove that the Earth was flat. We was kind of surprised to learn that we couldn't prove that it wasn't. If we stuck to the rule, and didn't use somebody else's conclusions, we couldn't prove much. I thought I had it when I mentioned that the Earth's shadow on the moon is circular, during a lunar eclipse. Jamie called foul, "How do you know that a lunar eclipse is the shadow of the Earth on the moon?" Me and Jamie had both watched an eclipse of the moon one night. It was a big event. Our two families got together for an ice cream supper before time for the Earth's shadow to touch the moon. Ma had showed me, in the encyclopedia, where to read about eclipses, so I could understand what was happening when the moon was looking so strange. I had thought I could use that, since we had watched together like we did. Of course, Jamie was right.

Try this: Is it right to eat meat?
Is it right for cows to eat grass?

When me and Jamie found out that we couldn't prove hardly nothing just by depending on what we had between our ears, we thought that maybe it was because we was so young and inexperienced.

I finally told Pa about our game. He said it was a sure enough grown-up kind of game we was playing. He said he thought we was pretty bright boys to be able to play. But he said that we might get ourselves on some dangerous ground by pretending that we didn't have good authority for our answers. Then he told me what the Bible says about not leaning on our own understanding.

I guess we would all starve to death before we could prove that it was alright to eat certain things. It's good that we have parents to tell us right from wrong.

Pa says that it ain't just young boys who come up with some pretty mushy ideas about what is right. Without no authority, what we call moral standards would be moving back and forth like ocean tides, except not nearly so predictable.

Me and Jamie still play our game some, for the mental exercise. The best part of our game is when it's over, and we leave the marshlands of uncertainty for solid ground.

Me and Jamie now sing with greater fervor, "Rock of Ages". We love our Rock. He is the solid foundation for our faith.

SKIPPING ROPE

I wouldn't want word to get out, especially over to the schoolhouse, but me and Jamie have started skipping rope. The girls at school have been skipping rope regular. Some of them have got plumb good at it. They will all chant silly little verses to keep the cadence and a kind of count – so that they can tell who can skip the longest without messing up. It's a girl's game. There are two games that girls play that don't seem silly to me: skipping rope, and hopscotch. The reason they don't seem silly is that they are not so easy to do.

Jack Dempsey skips rope, so I know it's alright for boys to do. What me and Jamie are concerned about is that we don't skip rope the way the boxers do, we skip rope the way the girls do. The way the girls skip is harder so it's more fun.

Jack Dempsey turns the rope hisself while he jumps. That's easy. Two girls will turn the rope while another girl jumps to their cadence. Once in a while two of them girls will jump at the same time. We make out that we ain't impressed, but we are. I wouldn't want a girl to know it but I just can't keep skipping without missing, like most of them can. I let on that I ain't interested in rope skipping – for them. I don't want them to know that it could enter my head to condescend to do it myself. None of us boys skip rope: not where no girls are likely to find out about it.

What me and Jamie do is to tie one end of the rope to a tree or a clothesline post, and take turns turning and jumping. We don't chant. We just turn and jump. To be perfectly honest, when I say we don't chant, I mean we don't make any sounds that the girls make. I couldn't hardly get started jumping until I started saying them chants in my mind. I ain't said nothing about it to Jamie, but I know he says them chants in his head too – I seen his lips moving.

I can't get as far as Jamie can. When I jump I don't quite get the table set. Jamie has got all the way to, "hot". Jamie says he could jump hot if I was turning the rope right. I do the best I can: "Ma-ble, Ma-ble, set the ta-ble. Don't for-get the salt and pep-per, vin-egar- hot…H, O, T." Before I spell, "hot", Jamie has always missed. I do my best to turn good for him, he already beats me so it ain't no competition. I sure do hate to think that neither one of us can get as far as Rosemary Raincamp does. She can get all the way through the chant at least once.

We don't mind Shirley knowing that we skip rope. Shirley skips with us. One of the best things about the rope games is that Shirley can always beat us. This is fun for all three of us. We just wouldn't want it to get out that we can be beat by a girl.

When we started skipping rope it helped to have Shirley play with us: she could help turn the rope. She could not turn for very long, though. We would soon have the rope tied to the clothesline post again. Few things we ever did seemed to make Shirley feel so much a part of things. I guess it had something to do with her besting me and Jamie.

We didn't say as much to each other, but I think both me and Jamie was delighted to be beaten at something by this particular girl. Aside from her being so lovable, Shirley didn't have many successes. She could jump rope almost as good as Rosemary – for a few turns.

The place where we tied our rope for skipping was in back of the house, away from the road. We didn't want nobody who had been at the springhouse to get an eyeful of scandal. Ma and Pa, Jamie's folks, Shirley, and Mrs. Peabody was the only ones we trusted with our secret.

We usually knowed when anything unusual happened, but one day Mrs. Peabody was to work only half a day and we didn't know nothing about the change. When Slim brought Shirley home from the Jackson's we was trying to improve our jumping skills. Slim saw us.

I can only try to explain how I felt when I saw Slim and realized that he had seen what we was about. Of all the boys I knowed, Slim was closest to my idol (maybe excepting Luther Murray, but Luther was much older). Slim could do about anything he tried to do, and what he did, he did well. Slim, home for a visit from Detroit, was looking after Shirley, already!

I knowed that boys was to do things different from girls. I loved Ma, but Pa was the one I wanted to be like. I wanted to grow up to be a lot like Pa – and some like Luther, and some like Slim. Me and Jamie was already one hundred percent boys. With the good examples we had, we was growing into men. Now we had been caught skipping rope! And by Slim Jackson!

Slim just waved at us and walked on to the Peabody house with Shirley. Me and Jamie sat down to rest a spell, and to try to recover from the shock of having been seen by our masculine mentor. (I went to the dictionary to find a word to help you understand how me and Jamie was feeling).

It wasn't just shame that had took all the starch out of our backbones. If Slim was to figure we was sissies, he wouldn't show us no more how to find the best wood for slingshot; how to jump over Hobson's creek; how to shinny up a tree; or how to do a hundred other things that girls don't do. The last persons I would want to think I was sissy would be Pa, or Jamie, or Luther, or Slim. Pa and Jamie knowed I wasn't sissy. But what was Slim thinking?

Me and Jamie was too upset to be talking these things over much, but we was both thinking along the same lines.

The pall that had settled over us was broken by Slim's voice. "Mrs. Peabody said it would be alright for Shirley to come over and jump rope".

As Slim spoke, Shirley was running ahead toward us, squealing excitedly, "Let me show you what I can do, Slim. Just watch".

Me and Jamie straightened up and untied the rope from the post so we could both turn for our friend. Even with the shame of seeming sissy in the eyes of our buddy, we wasn't going to fail Shirley. You just didn't refuse that lovable Shirley's simple request, when it clearly meant so much to her.

Slim watched Shirley miss a few times, then he said, "Let me turn one end of the rope." I handed my end of the rope to Slim and stood by as Shirley began to skip. Me and Jamie was amazed that Shirley got all the way to, "hot", before missing. It was time for her to rest. As she took a seat on the back steps, Slim gave the rope back to me and said, "Let me try it".

Slim can jump rope like nobody you ever saw. He is better than either Eleanor Crump or Rosemary Raincamp. He is better than anybody. It turned out that Slim had been jumping rope with his sisters since he was old enough to blow his nose. He was a natural.

The school crowd still don't know that me and Jamie skips rope. It ain't that we mind them knowing we would do it. Since we learned that Slim skips rope, we ain't worried about that no more. What we don't want them to know is that we have been practicing for months and still can't jump as good as a girl. We wouldn't want it to get out that Rosemary Raincamp could do anything better than us.

It might have something to do with the way girls are built – extra padding in places that gives them the balance for it – whatever it is – we can't play hopscotch as good as girls neither.

Now, do you believe I try to be honest with you?

But don't you dare tell. Rosemary and Eleanor are snotty enough, without you giving them no ammunition to blow our way.

HOUSEWORK

Every morning, about as far back as I can remember, Pa has got a fire started in the wood range, and Ma has breakfast well on toward ready to serve by the time I get to the table. After years of this happening a feller gets to thinking that it will always be so.

It ain't.

My whole world was changed for me one morning when Pa woke me and said I should go over to the Jacksons and fetch Maxine, if she could come. Ma was sick. Maxine was needed to help nurse Ma and to look after things about the house. I dressed in a hurry and ran to get the help Pa wanted.

As I ran, I thought how things was different. Ma don't get sick – Ma tends to others who get sick. If Ma is sick, I can't count on nothing no more. I tried not to worry, or to think thoughts that would get in the way of my prayers. I knowed that as soon as I could get the chance, I was going to lay down a real petition before the Lord. I didn't want to offend Him by my thoughts. You just can't find a way to hide nothing from Him.

I didn't want the Lord to hold it against me that I felt let down somehow that He had let my Ma get sick. I knowed that He knows best and that nobody should find fault with what He allows to happen. But why was my ma sick? If anybody deserves wellness, it's my ma.

The preacher says that prayer is a sincere desire of the heart. It was certainly my sincere desire that Ma get well quick. I wasn't praying exactly. I was just running toward the Jacksons and hoping that whatever the reason the Lord had for letting my ma get sick, He would get the job done quick and get things back to normal.

Mrs. Jackson invited me to have some breakfast. Even in my anxious state it took an effort to say, "No, thank you, Mrs. Jackson, I'd better get back and see how Ma is."

That Jackson kitchen sure did smell good.

Maxine didn't hesitate. She had already eaten her breakfast. We were back at the house in a short time.

Ma wasn't no better. Pa left Maxine and me to see after Ma and went to fetch Doctor Spoon. Ma had the flu. She was to be kept isolated as much as possible, and given plenty of liquids. She was to take aspirin. Mostly she was to stay in bed.

It was unthinkable! Pa had to insist on Ma staying in bed or Ma would have struggled to be up and about with her chores. Pa insisted that Ma follow the doctors orders exactly.

Maxine didn't go home that night. Slim brung some things for his sister to wear and she settled in for the duration of Ma's sick spell. The davenport in the parlor was prepared for her bed. Things was looking better.

Then Maxine come down with the flu.

On the third day after Maxine had come to look after Ma, Pa gave me breakfast and a mission. He said I should go tell Mrs. Jackson that Maxine was sick. He said, "Be very careful what you say and what you do. Don't go into the house. Stay back from anyone you meet. When her mother hears that Maxine is ill, she'll want to come to look after her. Tell her that the symptoms are the same as your mother's. Tell her not to come. She will probably insist on coming. If she does, tell her that I won't let her in the house. I'll look after Maxine and your mother. I can manage fine."

Pa took time to explain that because of the possibility of contagion, nobody else should be exposed.

I did my best to console Maxine's ma. Like Pa guessed, she thought she ought to come. That's the first time it looked like Mrs. Jackson might be mad with me. She acted less mad but still doubtful when I explained about the contagion part. Mas usually are plenty smart. When one of their own get sick, though, they think they ought to be with them no matter what. I don't think that's smart.

But, I'm glad I've got a ma who feels that way.

Like I said, my whole world changed. Pa did everything he said he would, except one: he looked after Ma; he looked after Maxine; he looked after me; but he didn't manage fine. By the time Ma got to feeling well enough to do for herself, Pa was tuckered – and so was I.

Ma was always a pretty woman. She never looked more beautiful to me than she did the day she came back to the kitchen and announced that she was ready to take over.

Breakfast sure was good that morning!

Ma had Maxine well in just two more days. Maxine stayed on with us for another week. We didn't want to take no chances with the flu spreading further. We would have kept our neighbor longer except for her and her ma wanting to get together again. Ma said, "Flu or no flu, you have to respect a mother's feelings".

The Lord don't explain all His reasons for what He does. Sometimes I reckon we try to guess what His reasons are. I know one good thing that I learned when Ma got sick: the dividing of things between man's work and woman's work has it's limits. A man can do what a woman usually does, and I've seen it work the opposite.

Another thing I learned is that there are things other than hopscotch and skipping rope that girls can do better than boys, especially when them girls is somebody's ma.

Raymond F. Rogers

SPRING HOUSE CLEANING

Since I know that a lot of folks who know about our springhouse might think I was talking about what me and Jamie do to keep baskets looking and smelling fresh, I want to say right off that that ain't it. It ain't about what Pa does to keep the water clear and pure neither. It ain't about the springhouse at all, so for this paper, just forget about the springhouse.

What this paper is about is the cleaning that takes place in that season of the year that is known as spring. There, I guess that should be clear enough. (Old Lady Showalter says we should make sure that a reader understands what we are writing about, right from the start. So you see why I didn't want you to get the wrong idea about what was being cleaned. When I said, "spring", I spoke of when the cleaning takes place, not what was cleaned.)

Maybe I should have just called this paper, "Cleaning In the Spring", but that title just didn't have the right ring to it. Besides, some of the good people who use our springhouse might be put off by the notion that we was taking baths in the cold spring water, or washing the dog there close to where the gourd dippers hang. Just in case this should be read by somebody with a weak stomach, let me assure readers that the spring water is fresh and pure. We don't even let Old Blue inside that springhouse, and he is as clean as a lot of the people who drink from the gourds.

Like I say, this ain't about the springhouse, so just forget it. I just wanted you to know that in case you was overcome by a powerful thirst for some of our cool spring water, there ain't no reason for you to be afraid to trust its purity.

Every year Ma takes down all the beds. We haul the slats and mattresses outside for beating and for sunning. While the beds, rugs and upholstered chairs are out drinking sunshine, we open all of the windows in the house and attack the fuzz balls, lint, cobwebs and such that have escaped the frequent "search and destroy missions" that Ma conducts with regularity.

If you was to watch Ma going about her regular cleaning chores, you wouldn't believe how many bits of fluffy lint and stuff is hiding out of her reach. Ma sees that these miscreants are purged from the premises at least twice a year. There just ain't no place to hide from Ma's spring house cleaning.

This paper ain't about the sunning and cleaning of the house and furnishings neither. I told you as much as I did about it, just so's you wouldn't think that it was neglected at our house. It wouldn't be fair to Ma if I left that impression. Ma keeps a clean house. Believe it!

This paper is about the kind of cleaning that would be the primary subject of complaint, if I ever was of a mind to complain about the way my ma runs things. Ma ain't satisfied to get at all of them little specks of dirt that can be seen. Ma goes after unclean things that she imagines might be hiding out of sight. Ma says that boys should be cleaned out on the inside. Just as surely as the house needs cleaning, boys need cleaning – inside and out.

Now, I don't mind that Ma uses strong Octagon soap, and heavy scrub brushes on the floors and in the corners of the house. I do protest the strong measures she takes to clean me out inside. Mind you, I don't sass Ma. I don't throw temper tantrums. (At least I don't do it no more. I tried it once; but Pa persuaded me, with logic and a leather strop, that temper tantrums ain't the right approach to solving no problems.) I admit, though, that I've tried to find other ways to avoid being voided.

I guess Ma discovered, years ago, that all of the furnishings that could be removed, should be taken from the house. That's the best way to be sure that all the little dust bunnies will be discovered and taken away.

I guess she figgered that boys should have everything removable taken out of them, too. Sometimes I've felt that, by the time Ma was satisfied that I was clean enough inside, I might be taken away.

What I've done was to hide the caster oil. Now, I know that children should obey their parents. It might look like to you that it was wrong of me to hide the caster oil. Before you judge me too harshly, let me ask you: have you ever tasted caster oil? Sometimes a feller just has to make a choice between two evils.

I thought I had found a perfect place to hide Ma's purgative. I hid it early in the spring before the sap started rising in the trees. I figgered that I was well ahead of Ma's spring annual crusade to make me pure within. I hadn't decided yet what I would answer when Ma asked me if I had seen the caster oil. I didn't think it would be too hard to avoid telling an untruth. I would probably say, "Yes, it was in there on the pantry shelf with the other medicines, when I used the iodine on my cut finger." Ma is so sympathetic to my hurts, she probably won't notice that I didn't say I hadn't seen the caster oil since.

What I did was to hide the caster oil in a hollow tree. The tree was back of the woodpile, well away from the house. I was careful to put the bottle far away from the opening so the sunlight wouldn't hit it and announce the presence of glass in the hollow.

I've told you about how Ma can deduce facts from slight evidence. It must be more than that. I've heard of woman's intuition. I don't know what it is. I just don't know how Ma knows almost everything I try to keep her from finding out about. Maybe mas have some kind of communication line that stays attached to their young, even after the umbilical is severed. (We read about kittens and puppies and babies, in the "Weekly Reader.")

Whatever uncanny gift she had, Ma found the caster oil. We was out early one morning to pick some wild strawberries. There wasn't no reason that I can think of why Ma would have noticed, in the early morning light, that it looked like the honeybees might have been working in that hollow tree. I thought that even when you noticed that bees was working someplace, you would allow them a little privacy, he will respect the bee's arsenal of defense enough not to go poking around where a whole swarm of them has decided to make a home.

Ma went almost as straight to that caster oil as if she had left the house for that purpose. I don't know how Ma found that bottle, but she wasn't about to believe that the bees had such a hankering for caster oil that they would organize a airlift to steal a bottle from her pantry shelf. Ma knowed at once that I had took the medicine. I knowed at the same time that I would have to take my medicine, and I ain't just talking about the caster oil.

211

Even fresh wild strawberries didn't taste good for breakfast. When Ma had made her discovery, she had just said, "Young man, you have some explaining to do."

If I had of knowed how the whole matter was going to turn out, I might have enjoyed my breakfast more. It has happened that I've been caught doing something I shouldn't have been doing, and I got a licking right away. What I had done this time was so plainly against my parent's will, that I expected to feel Pa's strop, and I didn't expect to wait long to feel the sting.

What I got was questions. Why? Why? Why? Ma and Pa also wanted to know how and when I had hidden the caster oil. Their main interest was in why I did it. I tried to tell them.

Last year, when they had had Mr. Detwiler, over to the drug store, fix me a orange juice-caster oil mixture, it had made me sicken at the very sight of a orange.

I had felt so nauseated that I had become tuckered by running to the outhouse so much.

Once, I had visualized myself becoming so exhausted that I lay on the privy path, turned wrong side out like a dirty sock. (This was laying it on a bit thick, but I wanted my folks to get the idea how much I loathed caster oil.)

Ma said, "Don't exaggerate, Frankie. Didn't you know that we would just buy more medicine if we couldn't find the old? Go do your homework, I want to talk with your father."

I had a hard time concentrating on plane geometry when the plain truth was I didn't know whether I would survive to turn my work in to the teacher. I knowed that Pa wouldn't give me that hard a licking, but I might be dissolved by caster oil. I was feeling a little like I might have already swallowed a dose of that greasy stuff, when Ma called me back to the kitchen.

Ma made me sit where I was looking at both Ma and Pa at once. "Frankie, you should never take it upon yourself to go against your parents. What you did was wrong. In spite of this, your father has convinced me that we should not force you to take the caster oil. Can you assure us that you will not be encouraged by this to defy us on other matters?"

I felt so relieved, that I barely answered, Yes, Mam." It looked like one of my ideas had worked almost as well as the caster oil.

I slept well. Breakfast this morning was delicious, with bacon and eggs, butter and jelly, hot biscuits and coffee. Coffee for a boy my age?

It was only the first part of breakfast that was delicious. The last part was coffee, mixed with Black Draught.

You may sometimes win, but you can't win them all!

I would tell you more, but, I gotta go!

GOAT CART

Usually, when there is a death in the community, folks will bring in plenty of pies and cakes, fried chicken, ham, roast beef, and other foods; so the cooks in the family where the death is, will not have to prepare meals through their tears, and there will be plenty to offer visiting relatives. Almost everyone tries to help members of a family to overcome their grieving.

After a little while, maybe a few days, there will be something else to happen in the neighborhood, and the care and attention will be directed toward someone else.

When Mr. Peabody died, it was different. Since Shirley was a special child, help was needed over a longer period. I don't know whether the grown-ups got together or not, to make sure that everyone was aware of the continuing need. I do know that a lot of people seemed to be always trying to find something they could do to help Shirley and her ma.

You know about some of the things the Jackson family did; and you know that Ma canned and preserved extra for them. I might not have told you that Mrs. Leonard and Mrs. Klinghopper did the same. Nobody made a big thing about it: they just did it.

Maybe one of the nicest things anybody did for Shirley took a lot of time to do. Old Man McElwaine made a goat cart for Shirley, and gave her a nanny goat to pull it.

I suspicion that one reason this was done, was so that there would be extra milk at the Peabody house. This was like adding a little extra income for the Peabody household; but it just looked like it was a special toy for Shirley's pleasure.

It was well known around the county that there wasn't nothing hardly that Old Man McElwaine could not do. He made cabinets and furniture, and kept a lot of automobiles going. I heard, over to the barbershop, that he could even make some of the spare parts for a Model T, or a Model A.

Once, when Ma was having circle meeting, and I was invited to have a piece of blueberry pie in the kitchen, while the ladies was being served in the parlor; I heard the ladies bragging that Mr. McElwaine must be very good with his hands. I had just finished my pie, and was walking past the parlor door, on my way back to my room when they was saying this. Two of them ladies was looking at each other like they had just pulled a good joke on Mrs. McElwaine. "It must be heavenly to be married to a man with such wonderful hands!" The way Mrs. McElwaine was blushing, she must have been embarrassed. It don't embarrass me none for folks to brag about my pa. I just don't understand grown-ups.

The cart that was made for Shirley had two bicycle wheels. They wasn't used wheels – they was brand new wheels that Mr. McElwaine had ordered from Sears Roebuck especially for the goat cart. Every thing else about that cart was shiny and new. It even had a cushioned seat for Shirley to sit on. The seat cushion had been made by Mrs. McElwaine and had a lace border around. Mrs. McElwaine had also made a little old-timey dress and bonnet for Shirley to wear when she rode in the cart.

Naturally the cart had to be small for a nanny goat to pull it, but it worked alright. The only thing was that Mr. McElwaine didn't know how to break a nanny goat to the harness. (It had a sparkling new harness, fitted to the small animal and cart.) The goat would pull well enough, but somebody had to lead the goat about to get it to go in the direction desired.

The way the gift was made to Shirley was kind of quiet, considering all of the excitement about it after the cart was seen in public. The Peabodys was invited to the McElwaines for supper. After the meal, the cart was presented to Shirley, complete with goat; and she was taken for some short rides about the McElwaine place, before riding it home for keeps.

Me and Jamie didn't play catch for a long time after that goat cart was give to Shirley. We would take turns leading that goat about for our little friend to enjoy her rides. Shirley never seemed to tire of her cart, but she would never complain when her ma would say that she had rode enough.

One day, when Mrs. Peabody had decided that Shirley should not ride but just a little while, me and Jamie asked if we could try to train Nanny to respond to the reins. We didn't have no bit in the goat's mouth, so it probably wasn't such a smart idea. We got permission, so we tried to train the goat.

Jamie got into the seat, while I led the goat. Jamie would say, "Right", and I would lead to the right; or he would say, "Left", and I would lead to the left. As Jamie spoke the directions, he also tugged the reins slightly to correspond to the directions spoken. After we had practiced with Nanny for a while, it seemed like she began to anticipate my lead, but I wasn't sure.

When we started to trade places, I was in the seat before Jamie had hardly got out. Nanny decided that this would be a good time to move out on her own. We had not set the brake on the cart, so me and Nanny and the cart were moving at a good clip toward the crossroads, before Jamie hardly knew that we had left him. I was having a good ride, so I just gave Nanny her head, or, since I couldn't have guided her if I had tried, you could say that I just determined to enjoy the ride. I rode to town.

You would have thought that Nanny must have seen a ad in the newspaper about a sale at Philpott's Seed and Feed Store. I could have put the brake on and stopped the cart at any time, so I was a little worried that Mrs. Peabody and Shirley would not be pleased with me about my joy ride.

Since I had a dime in my pocket, I was about to buy a dimes worth of oats for the nanny goat, when I thought about what she would do the next time she wanted something. I just set the brake and went to Nanny to try to coax her into starting back.

Earl Junior had run up behind us as we had arrived in the parking area of the feed store. I asked Earl Junior to release the brake, and I started back through the crowd towards home. I wondered if a traveling evangelist or somebody had come through to entertain the folks, until somebody said they were there to see the goat and cart. Me and Nanny had quite a following.

As much as I liked the attention, I didn't linger long. I had to get back with that rig to the Peabody's. I led a parade back to where Jamie, Shirley, and Mrs. Peabody were waiting in the yard. Soon, four or five cars followed those who had traveled on foot. A lot of people wanted to get a closer look at that little cart, and to take pictures.

We never did get to where we could count on Nanny to respond as desired to tugs on the reins, but she was kept pretty busy after school before supper time. Word about the rig spread until it seemed that everybody in the county must have had a peek at it.

Most folks don't want to appear immodest about their outstanding abilities; but I suspicion that they don't mind too much if strong clarion blasts announce their excellence, as long as they ain't blowing their own horn. Mr. McElwaine was soon famous for his handiwork.

Some of the merchants in Yanceyville wanted to show off their new clothes fashions by having a parade just before Easter. Shirley and her goat cart was to lead the parade. Mr. McElwaine at first said that me or Jamie could lead the goat, but, at last, he was persuaded to lead it hisself. Nobody deserved the honor more.

Shirley was dressed in her old-timey dress and bonnet, Mr. McElwaine dressed like the old pioneers. They were followed by a number of the local girls, who were dressed in the latest spring offerings at the stores. It was a small but beautiful parade.

Mr. McElwaine never gets much chance to rest up since that parade. He is always being asked to "please" make something or other for very particular people from all over the county, and beyond.

DEATH IN THE FAMILY

I know that not all people think like we do, but when I was born, my family numbered four. Before I came Ma and Pa and Old Blue was already a family. Ma told me that Blue didn't stay jealous of me for very long. He might even have helped me to learn to walk. We have been fast friends for as long as I can remember. I guess I would rather be hurt myself than to see Old Blue in pain.

Blue had been in a lot of pain lately. Doctor Hiram Sexton, the vet from over to Milton, said that there wasn't much we could do for Blue except to see to his comfort. I think that Ma and Pa have pretended that they were not so concerned for the dog, just to spare my feelings. They pretend: but I've seen the expression on Ma's face when she was smoothing Blue's blanket. I know that my parents love Blue, too.

If pats and hugs and words of affection can ease the pains of arthritis, Blue's last days were less troubled than they would have been otherwise. Our affections covered him more constantly than his blanket. In any case, Blue's aches at last dissolved into an endless sleep.

When some animals die, you just dig a hole and bury the thing, and that's the end of it. Blue was a member of the family: we had a funeral for him.

My folks are too devout to take funeral services lightly. They would not permit the same kind of service that would have been held for a human, who had declared his faith in the Lord. Old Blue had declared his faith plain enough, in his trusting eyes. But for all we knew, Blue's faith was in us; not in the Lord who opens His hand and "satisfiest the desire of

219

every living thing". Blue had such trust in us that he didn't think we would let him die. He didn't know that we couldn't keep him from dying, or promise him life after death.

Blue was to be interred in a place already prepared. Pa had mined about all of the light wood from the stump and roots of the yellow pine that had once stood near the Peabody line, at the edge of our cotton field. This left a large hole that would soon have to be filled anyway. This was to be Blue's final resting place.

Shirley wanted us to use the goat cart for the hearse. Pa made a box for the coffin. Ma wrote a eulogy. All of these things took place pretty quick after we found that Old Blue's stiffness wasn't due altogether to arthritis. You just don't wait long to bury an animal when the days are warm as it is just after Easter this year.

Ma's eulogy was about Blue's faithfulness, and about how thankful we were for being blessed to have his love and companionship. I would try to find a copy of what Ma wrote, so you could know her exact words; but I don't want to tear up again.

The funeral ceremony was all done quickly. I was trying hard not to cry in front of Jamie and Shirley, until I saw that they was weeping quite openly. Ma sobbed a little toward the end of her eulogy, and even Pa wiped away a tear. When me and Jamie was alone, while Pa was filling the hole where Blue's body was, we started talking about the resurrection. We wondered if Blue would be in Heaven. Jamie doubted if animals ever go to Heaven. I said I didn't see how it could be Heaven without Blue being there. We didn't settle nothing, but Jamie raised some interesting questions.

What do we really know? Do we know anything except what we've been told? Since we interpret our experience by information received through our five senses, can we be certain that we are not deceived by our senses into making incorrect judgments?

Now, Jamie ain't no older than me. How come Jamie knows enough to know that we don't know as much as him and me usually take it for granted that we know?

When it came time to answer Jamie, I had to admit that I wasn't sure of much. But I have faith. Faith can reach far beyond what may be certainly known.

I have faith that God will do what is best.

But I still don't know if I'll ever see Old Blue again.

THE CHRISTMAS APPLE

I guess I ain't knowed where babies come from long enough to be too much concerned about where teachers come from. I guess I ain't never thought much about it. Teachers just are: like death, and taxes, and chicken pox.

We learned a little about bees when we took a field trip over to the Pender Peach Orchard. I guess I just thought that, like there are worker bees, queen bees, and drones; there are working people, ruling people, and school teachers. I ain't thought much about where they come from. Some of them teachers look like they didn't come from nowheres. They have just always been, like stony faces in the everlasting hills.

Old Lady Showalter came from Greensboro. Ma told me that when my teacher was a little girl, she went to school at White Oak. This is where the cloth for my overalls was probably made. The mill in Greensboro ain't as close to our town as Haw River or Burlington, but I don't think it is very far.

How my ma got cozy enough with my teacher to find out where she came from is too long a story for one night's telling, but I'll try to let you know what happened.

Me and Jamie got kept after school. It wasn't to clean no blackboards and brushes neither. I was a little bit anxious about why she made us stay in. I didn't think she had seen me when I passed that note with a heart drawed on it, to Gladys Riddle. I couldn't think of nothing else I had done wrong, and I was pretty sure that Jamie hadn't done nothing he had got caught at.

Whatever we had expected – that ain't what it was. As soon as the other students had left the class and we couldn't hear them no more in the hall; the teacher had us come up nearer her desk, and to sit in the desks nearest to hers. I was just starting to think of the embarrassment of sitting at a girl's desk, when Miss Showalter said, "I think you two ought to know that I think of you as two of my better students. I think your close friendship is wonderful. Some of your papers have revealed things about your characters that I admire."

Now, I'll bet you thought I was going to say that she next said, "however", or "but." I sure thought that is what she would say. But she didn't!

When Miss Showalter talks to you, as close up as we was, she watches your face as you're watching her face. It seems like she can tell a lot about what you think of what she is saying. Anyways, right now she was looking at us like she was expecting one of us to say something. I couldn't think of nothing to say. "Amen", didn't seem quite right. Besides, I was still waiting for her, "however."

At last, she spoke again. "I wanted you to know that you are good students. I believe I know how you can be even better students. I have a plan that will involve your parents. I have written a note for each of you to take to your mothers".

Now, what would you have been thinking? Here we were, having just heard the teacher say what sounded like some very good things about us, but we was going to have to take home a note from the teacher. I still wasn't too thrilled at this idea. But when the teacher has already wrote a note for you to take home, there just ain't much choice left in it. We took the notes; gave a quick, "Thank you", and went straight home to get it over with.

That night Ma let me copy the note in Big Red. I'll tell you how Ma came to this decision later. Right now, I'll bet you want to get this note business over with too:

Dear Mrs. Friddle,

Your son, Frankie, is one of the most unusual students it has ever been my privilege to teach. He is obviously a very bright boy, but his progress in the use of proper grammar is far below the norm. As I have informed your son, Frankie is outstanding in many ways. Please contact me as soon as possible. I have a theory concerning how this situation developed, and a plan for improving the grammar. My plan will need your cooperation, as well as that of another parent to whom I am sending a nearly identical note".

That note has sure changed things. After me and Jamie's mas has met with Miss Showalter, both our mas is (are) paying a lot more attention to how me and Jamie says things (Jamie and I say things). I ain't supposed to say "ain't" no more. (I am not supposed to say, "ain't" no more. I ain't (I am not) supposed to use double negatives.. (Double negatives is that no nothing is something).

The worst part of this plan of Miss Showalter's is that I have to let Ma "monitor" my writing. Up to now, I don't think that Ma has been reading what I have wrote (written).

My big tablets was always out in plain view on my bookshelves, next to my Funk and Wagnall's. They was (were) kind of dog-eared from use, so you could tell that there was something written in them. In spite of this, I don't think that Mother had ever read them. They were private. They ain't private no more. (They aren't private anymore).

Ma (Mother) was good about it. She told me that she knew of the tablets and would like to read them, if it would be alright with me. She said that, if I agreed, I could read ahead of her and strike out, or remove from the tablets, any part that I might consider too private for her to see.

Now, I've had some feelings that I wouldn't want Mother to know about. She is probably a lot more understanding than most mothers, but, even so, I just don't want her to know some of my thoughts and feelings about girls. I don't remember ever getting so evolved with what I was thinking that I would have written too much about girls. Anyhow, I was glad for the chance to check.

Please excuse me if I wait until another night to finish this. It takes long enough to write something just because you have to look up what some words mean. When you have to watch out for grammar, too, it takes a lot longer.

I had already nodded off to sleep once without saying my prayers. When I did say them, I was so sleepy that I'd already asked the Lord to bless everybody before I remembered about the county sheriff.

I'm too sleepy to try to sort it out now. I know we're supposed to pray for all of them in authority. I didn't have no trouble with that when I hadn't even heard of that sheriff whose name I don't even speak. What do I pray for when I think of that hateful sheriff? When I ask the Lord to bless everybody, does the Lord pay attention to my words, or to what He knows is in my heart?

Well, even if I can't sort it out, I know the Lord can. I just hope I ain't done that mean old sheriff no favor.

Anyways, it seems like the reason I been using so much bad grammar is that I been too quick to write bad, like I talk. Ma's going to help me. I ain't going to do that no more.

CHANGES

Life sure does hold some surprises! I guess if somebody was to slip a alligator egg under a setting hen, she might be in for a bigger surprise than I got, but I ain't at all certain of it. My mother and Miss Showalter are as thick as peas on a knife that has been dipped in molasses. This all started when Jamie's mother and mine visited the school as Miss Showalter requested. This was strange enough, but you ain't yet heard my surprise.

Miss Showalter likes me! And she likes Jamie, too! The funny thing is; me and Jamie have to admit to each other that we have started to like her, too. I guess it's just hard not to like somebody when you find out that they think you're kind of special.

I know I might be taking a chance to even mention it in Big Red that Miss Showalter said something about me and Jamie that I wouldn't want to get out. I haven't even told Jamie. It ain't exactly the kind of thing you expect to hear about boys what ain't (are not) afraid to fight boys almost twice their size – that can throw a baseball so hard that other boys won't catch them without no extra padding in their gloves – that can skin their legs and be-hinds sliding into second, and not cry. Boys like that just don't want word to get out that the teacher thinks they are "precious."

It don't hurt either me or Jamie if the teacher thinks we are smart, or that we are generous and sharing. You'll understand that we neither one wanted to be no "teacher's pets."

After Miss Showalter, Mrs. Klinghopper, and Mother started their campaign to see that our grammar should improve, Jamie and I did start to say and write things better, but I don't' think it has helped us to sort things out in our minds no better. Maybe it will help us to think better when it becomes natural to talk like that without being so careful about it.

Mother got to liking Miss Showalter so much that she started telling Pa a lot about what she had learned of my teacher's early life. Pa never did act like he was bored with Ma's stories. I have seen him catch a wink or two while Ma was catching her breath between some of her longer recitals.

I don't know yet whether it was because of just friendship, or it was to help Jamie and me, or not, but Miss Showalter loaned Ma a school paper she had wrote while she was a student at the White Oak School in Greensboro. She said she had been reminded of her own work by some of the things that Jamie and I had wrote about sharing.

Since you aren't in love with me, like Pa is with Ma, you might find some of Ma's stories boring. I'll try to boil some of them down to the facts, so you can see how Miss Showalter came to write her school paper.

When she was in the sixth grade, Margaret Showalter had a crush on Claude Straughan. Claude was considerably older than Margaret and was already employed at the big denim mill at White Oak. Margaret thought that Claude had the bluest eyes, the handsomest face, the most gorgeous shock of wavy hair, and the sweetest disposition of any boy she had ever known.

Now, I know I don't look nothing like this feller must have looked, but the way Ma told about the way it was in the olden days when girls set out to get a boy's attention, it makes me almost scared just to think about it. Anyway, I better get on with telling what Margaret did to get Claude to notice her.

There was a bunch of things in the way of them two having a chance meeting. Margaret was an only child: no brother could bring Claude into the house. Claude was a Baptist; Margaret, a Presbyterian. She was a school girl, Claude had never even gone to school very much. Her father was an overseer. Claude's father was in charge of the carpentry shop at the mill.

Margaret Showalter asked for help.

They was planning a taffy pull at the new church parsonage at Buffalo Presbyterian Church. Since "Uncle" Billy Straughan, Claude's father was the builder of the parsonage; it shouldn't be out of the question for young Claude to be invited to the taffy pull. There were a lot of other boys in the Straughan family, and two girls. Margaret asked the pastor's wife to be sure that Claude and Ella Straughan were invited.

The taffy pull was to be on the same night of the last day of school before Christmas.

There was a lot to keep Margaret keyed up with excitement when the day came that her wishes might begin to come true. The weather was crisp, but not too cold, the teacher was altogether pleasant and beaming at the children as the gifts were being passed out. (These were gifts from the mill company, and had become a tradition). And, Margaret's chief rival had not come to school that day.

Infatuation can pull in strange directions. Before leaving the school building, Margaret stopped by the third grade classroom to take another look at the model of the school building. There was a scale model of the building, kept over from dedication day, that had been made from the architect's drawings. The fact that the model had been made by Claude's papa was enough to liven the girl's interest in it.

After a quick, wistful look, Margaret hurried toward home so fast that she overtook many of the smaller children, including Mattie Straughan, who was not exactly strolling, herself.

The White Oak Village was divided by the millpond. Many of the mill workers lived on the side of the pond opposite the mill. Since almost everyone walked to work every day, it was a great convenience that the company had erected a walkway across the millpond. The bridge was commonly called a gangway, maybe because it provided a way for a gang of people to get across the pond. It was a long way across that footbridge. Hundreds of people used that gangway every day. Margaret never did get used to crossing that bridge. She would get a little bit dizzy no matter whether she looked down through the cracks between the boards, at the side railing, or kept her eyes straight ahead. A lot of people said they were affected that way.

There was no question about anyone's safety, though. That bridge was built solid.

Margaret had passed Mattie just before she had neared the end of the gangway at 17th Street. Mattie had been holding her doll in her right arm, and her treat in her right hand. In her left hand, Mattie was holding a big, shiny, red apple. She was holding that apple at eye level as if to devour it with her eyes – or so Margaret thought.

Just as she stepped off the gangway, Margaret heard Mattie begin to cry. She turned to offer help to Mattie, but the weeping child ran by as if she couldn't see or hear anybody. Mattie's left hand now held her stocking treat. The red apple was gone. Mattie had dropped her apple! It had rolled under the railing, into the water, out of reach.

The girl who would grow up to be my teacher had mixed feelings. She was sorry that Mattie had lost her apple, but she was glad that she would have a good excuse to talk to Claude at the taffy pull that night. She knew that the young man who was so much in her dreams was especially fond of Mattie. No wonder Presbyterians believe in predestination!

It won't surprise you none to learn that I have not told this exactly the way it happened. This is mostly because I just don't know exactly how it all happened. By the time Mattie told Claude, Claude told Margaret, Miss Showalter told Mother, Mother told Pa, and I overheard it; some things is bound to get turned around a bit. What happened might not seem important to you. It was powerfully important to Mattie.

The weather that night was just about right for the candy making. The air was brisk, so the candy would not be too sticky for eager hands. It was cold enough for the inside of the house to seem cozy, but not so cold but that a couple could steal outside for a few moments of privacy. Margaret's excitement grew with the approaching darkness.

At the taffy pull, Margaret was careful to socialize with everyone, making sure she greeted each newcomer warmly. She had no intention of being obvious in the pursuit of her idol. She did not take the first lump of candy offered to her; Claude was occupied with a covey of Margaret's rivals. She waited until her chances had improved before she took a good sized piece of hot candy that had barely cooled enough to be gingerly handled. She went straight to Claude Straughan and asked his help in pulling the taffy. She said, "While we pull the taffy, I want to tell you about what happened to Mattie today." (I guess girls that are going to become school teachers are probably bolder than other girls).

Anyways, Claude buttered his hands good and they went outside on the porch to pull the taffy together.

Claude said it had been hard to console Mattie. She was still snubbing tears at supper time. What had so disturbed Mattie was not simply that she had lost the apple. She had lost the opportunity to present her mother with the finest fruit that she had ever held in her hands. All of the Straughan children loved their mother. Mattie had been excited by the rare opportunity to give her something so beautiful. The anticipation of pleasing her mother with so fine a present was probably what caused Mattie to be admiring the big red apple so as she walked home from school.

Pretty soon after the taffy pull, Claude Straughan married Emmie Swink. Margaret wasn't exactly crushed; there were other handsome boys around. Still she has not forgotten either Claude or his little sister. She was especially touched by the way the loss of her apple caused Mattie to reveal the depth of her love for her mother. The most handsome apple actually delivered into her mother's hands could not have told of her love so eloquently as did her tears at the lost opportunity.

"An apple for the teacher" has become so commonplace that the fruits no longer hold the fascination that they may once have held. They remain practical gifts because of their usefulness and the attractive wrapping that nature has provided for them. Miss Showalter has been presented with many such gifts, and has received them with gratitude. But each time she has held the fruit in her hands, she has remembered Mattie's efforts to award her mother. She always thanks the student, as she should because she is truly appreciative, but inwardly she adds, "But you wouldn't have cried, as Mattie did, if you had lost this apple".

THE LOVE APPLE

When Mother first read me the story that my teacher had written as a girl, I thought it sounded too much like Rosemary's papers. You could tell that they were written by a girl, or at least by somebody that wasn't concerned that he would be mistaken for a sissy. I told Mother that they sounded like Rosemary. Can you guess what she said? She said, "Good for Rosemary! Perhaps you should try to sound more like Rosemary, too. This is well written. You and I must work together to see that you no longer avoid good grammar. Boys should use correct English as well as girls. Wherever did you get the notion that bad grammar was a trait of masculinity? Your Father doesn't talk like that."

Mother waited for me to respond to her question. I was not able to answer. It had seemed so obvious to me that I hadn't even asked myself where the notion had come from. "Everybody knows that no boy ought to sound like a girl talking". I knew that this was no answer. It didn't even satisfy my own mind. Mother would never buy it. "Let me think on it some, Ma. I'll try to speak better just because you say I should". That was the best I could think to say. It seemed like my mother had gotten a lot rougher with me since she had been talking to my teacher.

"Frankie, please believe that you should learn to speak well for your own good. Already you are writing with imagination and interest. You may become a real writer, if you learn correct practices. Wouldn't you like to copy Miss Showalter's composition? It may help you". Mother can be persuasive. I would have copied the paper just because she said I should; but she wanted me to believe that it would help me.

LOVE APPLE

By

Margaret Showalter, age 13

Excitement was rising in Mattie's heart faster than the sun was rising over the picnic woods. This was a very special day: the last day of school before Christmas.

On most of those crisp winter mornings Mattie and Marvin, the eight year old Straughan twins, were loath to leave the cozy warmth of the big kitchen of their house on Twentieth Street. Even on this day, they did not leave before they had eaten plenty of warm biscuits, bacon, and eggs, with milk; which was the usual fare. They just ate more hurriedly today. And today, they did not envy five-year old Clarence the privilege of staying in the comfortable room with Mama and two-year old Charlie. Even the almost perfect atmosphere of Mama's kitchen was insufficient to lull them away from the great expectations of the things that awaited them at school.

It was the custom for the Cone Mills to provide all of the students in the company schools with a gift and a treat of nuts, fruits and candies at Christmas time. A special gift was chosen for the boys in each grade, and another for the girls in each grade. Sometimes the children could guess what their gift might be, by assuming that they would be the same as the gifts for the same grade in prior years. This did not still the excitement; it often served to enhance it.

In a large family like that of the Straughan's, it was expected, with the expectation encouraged by a firm mama's hand, that treats of candy and

Raymond F. Rogers

such would be shared among siblings. Mattie was looking forward to sharing hard candy with Clarence and Charlie. She was especially pleased to think that she might find something special to give to Mama. And, she might have a doll for herself!

"Oh, please hurry, Marvin! Can't you see that you have your coat buttoned wrong?" Mattie was impatient to get the walk to school underway: down the path between the houses on Nineteenth, Eighteenth, and Seventeenth Streets; across the long, railed footbridge that spanned White Oak Pond; on up Sixteenth Street and across the railroad bridge to the new brick schoolhouse.

To Mattie, it was important to learn as quickly as possible what her gift would be. It was even more important to rush home with her present to show it to Mama and to her two younger brothers. Uppermost in her mind was the hope that there would be a big red apple for her to give to Mama. Their Papa always brought a barrel of apples for Christmas, but they were not the kind of big red apples that they usually found in their treats at school.

By the third grade, each of the children had come to expect that, in addition to the nuts and candy, each treat would contain a cluster of raisins, an orange, and a big red apple. It was the big red apple that had Mattie so keen with excitement. This was to be her special gift to Mama.

Mattie was happy that she did receive a doll. She was pleased with her fruit, nuts and candy, all contained in a mesh stocking treat. She was enthralled by her apple; it looked perfect. She had expected a good apple; this kind of beauty in one fruit was more than she had dreamed.

Mattie hardly knew what else went on in school that day. Her excitement had climbed to euphoria by the time school was out and she was able to start home. She gave little thought to her twin, Marvin who was in another class. She didn't know, or care much, what Marvin would do with his things. The important thing now was to get her prize to Mama.

The happy little girl didn't think of herself as over-burdened with her treasures as she hurried on down Sixteenth Street toward home. She held her doll in her right arm and carried the well-stuffed stocking in her right hand. In her left hand she held her pass to perfect pleasure. She could almost see Mama's pretty dark eyes shining as she was presented a gift of such perfection.

Once in a while, hardly noticing that she was making the adjustment, Mattie would kind of hitch the doll up to restore it to the position in the crook of her arm from which it had slipped slightly. Her thoughts and her eyes were mostly on what she had for Mama. Oh, why couldn't she walk faster?

The walk across the footbridge had become almost routine. Mattie no longer became dizzy because of the tricks her eyes would play on her as she moved across the many boards that formed her path. Today she kept her eyes pretty well fixed on the finest fruit she thought she had ever seen.

As our little heroine neared the end of the bridge, she heard the sound of footsteps overtaking her from the rear. The bridge was plenty wide enough to allow someone to pass: she moved slightly toward the right railing as Margaret Showalter hurried by.

She was becoming aware that the doll had slipped just a little lower in her arm. As she started to make the almost automatic little hitch to get a better grip, she felt if slip further. In making her recovery, Mattie somehow relaxed the hold on her apple: it dropped. She watched helplessly and disbelievingly as her prize rolled away from her, under the railing, and into the water. It was out of reach – gone!

It may have taken Adam a while to realize what he had lost when he was banished from Eden. So vivid had been Mattie's dream of presenting the perfect gift to Mama, she knew at once when the apple dropped into the water – this was paradise, lost.

Is it any wonder that she cried?

TOUGH TALK

I know you'll be glad that I finally bought a art gum eraser so you won't have to see so many of my mistakes. It is hard to write what you think, when you are thinking in one language, and writing in another. Anyways, you won't see all of my mistakes anymore. When I first started to make entries in Big Red, using grammar that Mother would not find fault with, I quickly used up the erasers on all my pencils. This made the pages ugly with smears as well as with errors. That's why I had some words down both ways. I knew it was hard to read so I changed. I aim to please.

I promised Mother that I would try to explain why I persisted in speaking and in writing poor grammar for so long. I could not answer at once, because I really didn't know. I searched my head for an answer and found none. I may have found the answer in my heart. It might be correct to say that part of the reason may be found there. I couldn't think of any good reason to talk like I did, until I realized that my efforts to change were making me feel disloyal to some old friends.

Mother left me feeling torn, when she asked why I did not follow my dad's example in my speech. Why indeed? My father is the one I want to become most like; but, as I've mentioned before, I want to be some like Slim Jackson and some like Luther Murray.

I still can't shake the feeling that any attempt to use better grammar, is an attempt to sound more like Rosemary Raincamp. This makes me feel disloyal to Jamie and to Luther.

You may have forgotten about Luther. I could never forget him. Luther was much older than the other students in our school. He was ten years old before he came to school at all. He was large, even for his age, but he was kind to all the smaller children. We loved him, but we wouldn't have dared to think of our affection as love. We admired Luther's ability to influence others. Luther never attempted to speak correctly. To speak like Luther was to support him. He was a strong, capable citizen in the things that mattered. I think it was easy to continue this pattern when Luther married and moved to Danville. It sounded tough to use the grammar Luther used.

I am not sure that this is all the answer. It is not easy to admit that laziness was another part. To give an example: I have spent more time on this one page than I used to spend on three pages. It takes real effort to do things according to rules. It is especially difficult when the rules are not respected. Until quite recently, I have had little reason to change my regard for the rules of grammar. Mother and Miss Showalter are determined to change that. I aim to please.

You have changed! Don't be alarmed by my observation. This is part of my explanation for the changes in my speech and writing. I started addressing my remarks to a different person. It works.

I used to write for myself alone. This was dull. It helped in my school work, but it was little fun. Then I started, almost unconsciously, to address imagined readers. I wrote a lot to Luther. I wanted Luther to know what happened here since he left, and I wanted him to be proud of me.

Some of my writing has been addressed to the readers of "Liberty". Someday a young boy may go to the barbershop and sell a magazine with one of my stories in it. When you fantasize, anything can happen.

Most of my writing will be for readers who like to listen to Rosemary's papers. The only reader I'm sure of is Mother. If I should slip and put in a double negative, consider it a tribute to my friend Luther Murray. Luther is a fine man, and my friend. I don't care if he never learns good grammar, he will be held in no less esteem by me and Jamie.

Raymond F. Rogers

GRANGE MEETING

I haven't been writing in my Big Red tablets for a long time. Just before writing this, I began looking over some of the things that were written long ago. I wrote some pretty candid stuff that makes me wonder just how I was able to be so straightforward.

One of our poets has remarked that the child is father to the man. I think that in my early entries in these tablets, I imagined that the me doing the writing was addressing the me I would grow up to be. I think that is a more complete explanation than just to say that I was writing to myself. If, in these tablets, the child was writing to the man, I will soon be ready to begin reading them in earnest. I am growing up fast.

I guess one reason for my neglect of writing is that I would be ashamed to put down all of the thoughts of a boy growing into manhood. Even if the words were to be kept private for my reading alone, I wouldn't want to be reminded of them. If I could keep some of my thoughts from God, I think I would do so, provided that this occasioned no offence; and if the rehearsal of those thoughts were not necessary to earnest prayer. I need forgiveness: then I would like to forget the thoughts.

As I write, I am consciously using a device I had almost forgotten. I address an imagined reader, as well as my future self. This requires a greater discipline of expression than would simple notes for ready reference. It also helps me keep my thoughts in order. Even as I use this device as a help I know that many ideas fail in expression partly due to the ambivalence of feeling the writer experiences in trying to distill thoughts into words. To put it more simply: sometimes I can't say what I

242

mean, because I am not sure myself. I feel I almost know. Many thoughts can be expressed in words; if there are words for all my thoughts, those words are not in my vocabulary.

In the past few months, my whole being has been engulfed in tides of feeling which were much stronger than my prior experience had prepared me to expect. I do not say that I had not been told to expect such feelings: I had been forewarned. I have been amazed at the strength of those tides; or of my desire to ride upon those tides, like a surfer rides a surfboard on rolling ocean waves.

But I have been warned that these are treacherous waters, which beguile novices into taking risks which could expose them to the breakers of heartache, or to the undertows of ruined lives. I have not taken to surfing, but I feel as though I might be a cork, afloat on strong, compulsive tides.

Gladys is my girlfriend. We have been close for several years. She is attractive and sweet. It is a delight to dream of the day when Gladys may be my wife. But the day of which I dream is distant; and I have a present surging desire which the dreams of distant days cannot assuage. My purpose to honor my future wife remains constant. It is my feelings which drift like a cork upon the ebb and flow of my hormonal changes.

Gladys and I have learned a lot together. We are together in school classes often, and in the Baptist Young People's Union, as well as the times we make for ourselves. We have the advantage of maturing as a pair, rather than separately, as most couples must. I can think of no better conditions under which I could await the time for Gladys and me to be married – still it is unexpectedly difficult to cope. I can think of no excuses to offer that it should be so difficult for me. If I was as honorable as the little boy who wrote in these tablets, it should be easy. It is not. It is not easy at all!

Jamie and I went, without female companions, to the Grange picnic. It is rare these days for us to go out together like that. Gladys had been expecting me to ask her to go with me, and I knew it. I knew that she would be hurt that I wanted to go without her, but I persisted, having only a vague notion of why I chose to go without her. She didn't have to go everywhere with me!

It was at the picnic that I met Deloris. Deloris is one of those girls who quickly catch your eye, even when you are in the presence of your chosen lady. To the unattached couple at the picnic, she looked gorgeous. The only thing that prevented Jamie and me from engaging in a contest for her attention was that she had a female companion who held Jamie's interest. The two girls were as ready for new acquaintances as were we. Looking back on it, I guess you could say that they were easy pick-ups. It just doesn't seem fair of me to suggest that they were in any way responsible for Jamie and me forgetting our relationships with the girls we had left at home.

We were invited by the new girls to share their lunches with them. With every bite we took we became more convinced that the invitations would be extended to take much more. Such tempting delicacies were not easily refused. We separated to taste desserts.

Until now I had never engaged in the kind of activity for which I was headed. I believe the term for the kisses and hugs I exchanged with my warm and eager new acquaintance is "heavy petting". I found Deloris to be as soft and yielding to my touches as I had imagined her to be. Soon I had explored her softness into regions where I had never ventured with a girl before. My only previous experience was with someone who was more careful of the bounds of propriety. (Gladys would have stopped me long before I had reached this last pulsating goal).

We were in an isolated place, near a lake, in a small cove. There was a boat nearby that helped to shield us from the view of the casual after-picnic strollers.

I was thoroughly enjoying the exploration of delightful feminine turf, when I was startled out of my engaging activity by a question. Deloris asked, "Did you bring any protection?"

There is a Latin phrase that ends, "……..interruptus". If Deloris had not spoken to interrupt us, I am not sure what might have happened. In fact, it was a few moments before I realized that our activities were more restricted than I expected them to be. I can claim no credit for controlling the situation. To me, control was lost. Fortunately for me, when I realized the significance of the question Deloris had asked, desire began to ebb.

A gentleman is careful with a lady's feelings. When Deloris suggested that I make a purchase at a nearby drugstore, I walked with her, around the lake to the store she suggested. She waited outside while I went into the store.

I have had no experience in making the planned purchase, and was wondering how to phrase my request for service, when I noticed that the clerk had run outside to confront Deloris. They were arguing so heatedly that they could be heard through the storefront windows.

Suddenly I realized that I had been used! But what a relief it was to be off the hook. All of the way, as we had walked to the drugstore; in my mind I could see the hurt look on Gladys' face. I had no wish to injure my beloved. Oh, how close I had come!

I still find continence to be difficult. I remain under the influence of the surging tides, as before. But now I know more of how strong the urges can be. I wade in the shallows, away from deep water, in the company of my beloved Gladys.

You will understand, now, if I do not make you privy to my prayers. Only God knows some of the things I refuse to share merely to provide entertainment.

SENIORS

Jamie and I moved on up into Miss Ophelia Clark's room in the fall. We were both saddened, that summer had to end, but we were happy, too. There are times when a fellow feels two ways at the same time.

It may be part of growing up, but I have even noticed that my earlier remembrances of Miss Showalter must have been colored by my youth. She is really quite pretty, in a mature sort of way.

Jamie and I aren't seeing as much of each other as we did when we were younger and more carefree. I see Gladys Riddle much more often than I do James now; although he and I do fish together at Mabry's millpond. When we have a good catch we will usually, but not always, be together for the subsequent fish fry.

James Klinghopper and Nellie Blake are, as they say, an item now. When I first started doing homework with Gladys, and going to picnics with her, Jamie seemed to be a little put off by it. We stayed pals, though, and it wasn't long until he had taken sufficient notice of how Nellie was developing, that there was no problem at all.

I am hesitant to try to tell how I feel about Gladys. I am inhibited, partly by a lack of skill of expression, and partly by a feeling that if I should become too candid, it would be a violation of her privacy.

My feelings about the world, my devotion to God and country, and my approach to problem-solving, have all been greatly affected by my close association with Gladys. The people at church say that even my speech has changed.

Raymond F. Rogers

I feel incomplete when I am not in the presence of my beloved and I yearn for her. When I am with her, I ache with a longing that is only partly soothed by the sweetness of her understanding. I grow stronger in her presence with my desire to protect her and to provide for her future happiness. Anyone who has had a similar experience will recognize that I am in love. Anyone who hasn't felt as I feel cannot be made to understand the urgency I feel for the time to pass quickly until we can be married – and there is still another year before I am even out of high school!

Gladys says that she knows I will like Miss Ophelia Clark. Gladys has worked with Miss Clark in a journalism class and getting the yearbook together. Such work is usually the province of seniors but Gladys has advanced skills in communication and was able to work with the seniors last year.

I look forward to this year's studies with a great deal of pleasure. I want to work hard to become better able to take care of Gladys.

There has been a great deal of talk in the Methodist church about their new preacher. Gladys has a friend, Lois Tippet, who works at the County courthouse in Yanceyville and is a member of the Methodist church. Gladys and Lois did some research together in the school library at Yanceyville and talked about a number of things of interest to them both. (Other women might have been gossiping.) Some of the church members fully expected the church organist to land a good catch with the preacher; but he is known to come into Yanceyville so often that some of the church people thought he might be neglecting some of his duties to the congregation. Lois said she had it as a fact that the young Methodist preacher was dating steady a woman in the Yanceyville community, and, further, this woman is a Presbyterian and somewhat older than the young man!

The picnic table on the school grounds was really abuzz with excitement among all the teachers today. Miss Showalter is sporting a new diamond ring!

It turns out that Miss Showalter had planned to wait for the announcement, but she will have to leave the school because her fiancée is being transferred out of the county.

Miss Showalter will become Mrs. Widenhouse as the young Methodist minister begins his work at a new church!

I hope you enjoyed our little talk. If you're ever in Caswell county, stop by our springhouse for a dipper of good, cool water; and come on up to the house and say hello to Mother. I probably will not be home.

GOLD STAR

Jamie and I volunteered for the Army Air Force during WWII. We wanted to stay together and be airplane mechanics, but Jamie qualified in skeet shooting and was off to gunnery school. In a few weeks he wrote that he had made staff sergeant and would soon leave the school in Florida. We both knew that he would most likely go to England.

I didn't even get a letter from Jamie after that. I learned later that he had been lost, with the rest of his crew, somewhere over Germany. He was a tail gunner on a Liberator Bomber.

When the war was over, I felt almost guilty about being happy to get back to my wife and two daughters. It seemed unfair; somehow, that I was all in one piece while Jamie and thousands of others would not be returning at all.

When I went to call on Mr. and Mrs. Klinghopper, I know they were glad to see me. They had that star in the window and a big picture of Jamie in the parlor. He was smiling that wavery smile and was showing his sergeant's stripes. Jamie's mom and dad both shook my hand real firm – and then gave me a big hug. I knew that they had to be thinking of the awful price they had to pay for us to be at peace again. They had to wonder why it was me back and not Jamie. I couldn't stay long.

I still don't understand it. It seems so unfair that Jamie, and so many like him, had not returned. Jamie was as deserving of happiness as anyone I ever knew, and he hadn't even lived to taste the joys of married life. Mr. and Mrs. Klinghopper were left without an heir. I was no more deserving and had two beautiful daughters already, with another package promised.

Oh, the hatefulness of war! Such a terrible price to pay because of the criminal acts committed against a people thousands of miles distant. But we would do it again. Oh, the horror of it! Jamie and millions of others have died, yet we may have to do it again.

I can't fish anymore with Jamie. We won't play marbles, or catch, or mumblety peg, or kick the can. But I'll see him again.

You see, the Lord loves Jamie, too.

About the Author

Raymond F. Rogers was born in Greensboro, North Carolina in 1923, and served in the Army Air Force during W.W.II and the Postal Service later, retiring in 1979 as a postal supervisor. He has four children, Marian Knight, Carolyn R. Williams, David Richard, and Kenneth Raymond. They all have children of their own. Beginning his efforts to become a published poet after the death of his father in 1985, he has since been honored to read at the Fields of Earth Symposia, winning the Max Vestal Memorial award three times. Encouraged by the public readings he began submitting his work to other publishers. These gave further encouragement, he is now a member of several poetry organizations The National Author's Registry, Poertry.com, and The International Society of poets. A sample of his poetry may be read on the Internet. Just get on Poetry.Com and follow instructions.

Shortly after obtaining an Epson computer sometime in 1988, he wrote a history of his childhood. Publication of the whole seemed impossible so he limited publication to the times he visited the farm of his father's parents. His small book was published in 1992. *My Childhood's Eden* was the only book he published until he won the poet of the year prize, part of which was publication of the chapbook entry, *Walking in Another 's Shoes*. This was followed by *Happy Ever After,* a tribute to his wife.

Me and Jamie was the most fun to write but harder to sell, possibly due to its honestly horrendous grammar. The writer could hardly expect more, but he believes that wisdom can and exists, quite apart from academic learning! The book could be helpful in demonstrating that correct use of the educated tongue is prerequisite to economic success. The writer believes it could be useful in closing the gap in the academic testing recently given. He believes that wisdom exist among completely uneducated people.